CONTENTS

Foreword

Francis Hacker is regarded by many historians and commentators as one of the villains of the English Civil Wars. Yet, in my opinion, the claim couldn't be further from the truth.

He is indeed one of the men who signed the execution warrant of the tyrannical King Charles the First, and he was certainly a soldier of fearsome repute on the battlefield. This latter point is the reason the King offered Francis command of one of his cavalry regiments when he attempted to persuade the Parliamentarian officer to swap sides midway through the first war. Unsurprisingly, Francis declined, choosing imprisonment rather than duplicity.

There is no doubt Francis was a flawed man who often made mistakes. But to write him off as a fanatic of the Puritan regime (as many do), and someone who did the bidding of his master, Oliver Cromwell, without remorse or conscience, is stretching things too far. For Francis was, more than anything else, a man of principle who regularly displayed great courage – and repentance. And he was most certainly a product of the powerful and wealthy family he was born into.

In my opinion, too little has been written about the Hacker family in the years since 1660, when Francis met an untimely death at the end of the hangman's noose at Tyburn. It is easy to understand why: the Restoration of that year saw a revival in royalist fortunes and reputation, and ever since there has been a reluctance to cast Cromwell and his lieutenants as heroes when it is far easier, and convenient, to blacken the names of men who fought for a cause they believed was just and godly.

Thankfully, Catherine Pincott-Allen's new research into the Hacker family, who resided in Stathern, East Bridgford and Colston Bassett, helps fill the void.

Catherine's book is an illuminating and fascinating read. It corrects many mistruths and misperceptions about one of Nottinghamshire's most prosperous families of the Sixteenth and Seventeenth centuries, and identifies some illuminating facts about Francis's ancestors, direct family members and descendants. It most certainly paints an absorbing picture of bygone times that helped to shape modern Britain.

The Hacker name may be one that continues to divide opinion in the modern day, particularly in Nottinghamshire and the Vale of Belvoir. But thanks to the work undertaken by Catherine Pincott-Allen, the life and deeds of Francis Hacker, the regicide, can now be put into a wider context and be understood more completely.

As someone who is fascinated by this rich period in our history, I am extremely grateful for this valuable and insightful contribution.

Philip Yorke

2023

A Further Account

of

The Hacker Family

By Catherine Pincott-Allen

A Field Detectives' Investigation 2023
Revised March 2024

First published in Great Britain in 2023

Second Edition March 2024

© The Field Detectives 2023

Lost Voices Publishing

ISBN 978-1-7385568-0-9

www.the-field-detectives.com

Preface

This particular project began in Stathern, Leicestershire when the Field Detectives started investigating the mill at the top of Mill Hill and the family of millers who lived and worked there during the 19th century. Our enquiries led us to a group attempting to save the Red Lion public house at Stathern, where it was reputed that village resident, Colonel Francis Hacker, had signed the death warrant for King Charles I in 1649. As legends go, there is usually some truth in a story, and such is the case with this one. The death warrant was signed in London, but Francis did keep it at his home in Stathern for about eleven years, unsigned by him but pivotal evidence in his demise.

The Hackers were a significant and wealthy family in Nottinghamshire, and Colonel Hacker's relationship with Oliver Cromwell and his intense involvement in the English Civil War played a major part in the shaping of 17th-century England.

Along our research path, we met author Philip Yorke, who is writing a series of five novels about Colonel Hacker and the English Civil War. Rebellion and Redemption, the first two books in the series, are already available and are unmissable reads for anyone interested in this era of history.

Our fascination for Francis Hacker grew, and the family history research even more so. The challenge of finding records from the early 17th century and the Commonwealth Gap all added to the intrigue of this influential family.

Many accounts of the Hacker family tree exist, written and online, and many more myths and legends exist around them. This booklet attempts to unravel these myths and legends, search for the truth and bring them together in one definitive place.

A much-used reference for early genealogy is the Visitation of Nottinghamshire 1662 by William Dugdale, Norroy King of Arms, in which two Hacker pedigrees are recorded. An important initial source for my research was a paper titled 'Some Account of the Hacker Family' by A.E. Lawson Lowe F.S.A. found in the book *Old Nottinghamshire* edited by J. P. Briscoe 1881, in which Lowe describes various branches of the Hacker family tree. Another was an essay entitled *'Colonel Francis Hacker, parliamentarian and regicide'* by H. Leslie Hubbard, 1941. It was the winner of the Robert Mellors Prize at the University of Nottingham. Hubbard references Briscoe but delves deeper into the life of Colonel Hacker and a search for his place of abode in Stathern.

All are detailed and informative accounts outlining the Hacker genealogy, however, with the multitude of online records now available to explore, as my research continued, the more I began to question some of the lineage recorded. Determined to put the story straight, this is our 'Account of the Hacker Family', which mainly follows the lineage of Colonel Francis Hacker's ancestors and descendants.

This is not a critique but a review of the earlier work done now that more research resources are available.

Catherine Pincott-Allen

2023

Introduction

History is forever being rewritten as new research comes to light, and this has been the case with our continuing search for Stathern Hall, Leicestershire, the home of Colonel Francis Hacker. Stories are told, legends grow, and over the years they become facts, but among them there is usually some grain of truth.

Search the Internet for what happened to Francis's home after he was executed, and you will be informed that his estates were forfeited by King Charles II and given to his brother James, the Duke of York, and that Stathern Hall was demolished. Some say that the village wanted to wipe out any memory of a regicide having lived there, or that locals pulled it down and recycled the stone for buildings in the village. Confiscated by the crown Francis's estates certainly were, and his brother Rowland was indeed able to buy back some of the properties, including those at Colston Bassett and East Bridgford, Nottinghamshire. However, we have been unable to find any documented evidence to say that Stathern Hall was ordered to be demolished. In fact, our recent findings have brought to light that the estate on which 'The Hall' was said to stand was a leasehold farm of eighty acres, on which records suggest stood a house rather than a hall. Following Francis's death, the lease expired on the farm, and by 1662, it was held by the Earl of Rutland.

In the area where the house or hall is reputed to have stood, there is no visual trace of a building, nevertheless, the Field Detectives have recently re-visited the geophysical survey carried out by the Framland Archaeology Group (FLAG) in 2001 and 2005 and expanded the search grid. Their findings supported those carried out by FLAG, and it is hoped that further study in the area can be continued in 2024. The report can be found on our website - www.the-field-detectives.com.

My passion for genealogy and filling in gaps in family trees had already led to finding Colonel Francis Hacker's birthdate, and that his father had a first wife, thus correcting previous beliefs that he was born in 1618. However, the new research has unearthed other discoveries, and alongside our latest findings relating to Francis' home, his chapter has been particularly revised. I hope that you will be as fascinated by the Hacker family and the turbulent times in which they lived during 17th-century England as we are.

Catherine Pincott-Allen
March 2024

THE HACKER FAMILY

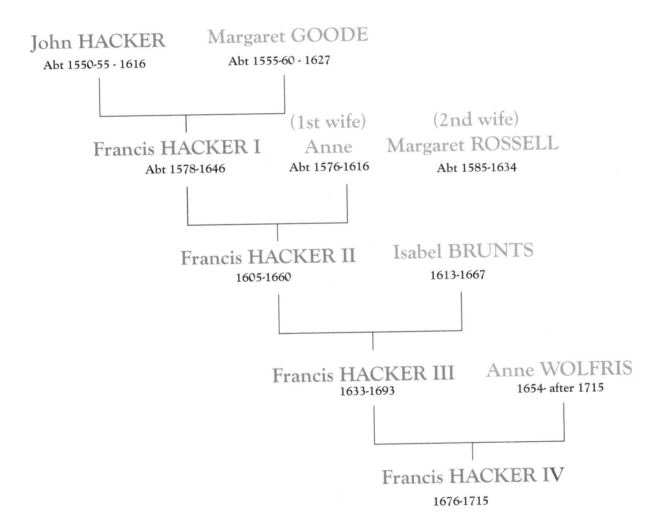

John HACKER
Abt 1550-55 - 1616

Margaret GOODE
Abt 1555-60 - 1627

Francis HACKER I
Abt 1578-1646

(1st wife)
Anne
Abt 1576-1616

(2nd wife)
Margaret ROSSELL
Abt 1585-1634

Francis HACKER II
1605-1660

Isabel BRUNTS
1613-1667

Francis HACKER III
1633-1693

Anne WOLFRIS
1654- after 1715

Francis HACKER IV
1676-1715

The **Hacker** Family

John Hacker I Full name of Husband	Solicitor & Man of Business	Abt 1550-55 Yeovil, Somerset Birth Date and Place
Unknown His Father		Calculated 1575-8 Marriage Date and Place
Unknown His Mother with Maiden Name		29 Mar 1616 St Peter's, East Bridgford Burial Date and Place
Margaret Goode Full name of Wife		Abt 1555-1560 Bassingbourn, Cambridgeshire Birth Date and Place
Thomas Goode Her Father		
Clemens Her Mother with Maiden Name		6 Jan 1627 St Peter's, East Bridgford Burial Date and Place

And The Children Were...........................

1. Francis I	Born: abt 1576	Married: [1]Anne abt 1597 [2]Margaret Rossell née Whalley 23 Dec 1617 East Bridgford	Buried: 20 Jan 1646
2. Luce	Born: abt 1576-79	Married: William Mayfield Abt 1597 ?East Bridgford	Buried: 3 Jun 1637 Lucia wife of William, E.B.
3. John II	Born: abt 1580	Married: [1]Catherine Tevery [2]Margaret Warbourton (widow)	Died: between 1625-1644
4. Rowland I	Born: abt 1582-84	Married: [1]Barbara Poole 5 Sep 1603 Barrowby, Lincs [2]Elizabeth Yarborough (widow) 6 Feb 1636, London	Buried: 4 Apr 1639 East Bridgford
5. Richard	Born: 1586 Hardwick, Derbys	Married: [1]Alice Hill [2]Katherine Ballard [3]Anne Wood	Died: 1654
6. Marie	Born: abt 1589-90	Married: John Day 19 Jun 1617 Wysall, Notts by licence	Died: Unknown
7. Elizabeth	Bapt: 25 May 1593 East Bridgford	Married: [1]Thomas Wightman 9 Jan 1613/14 E.B. by licence [2]Richard Harpur of Littleover, Derbys abt 1616	Died: Unknown

Most ages are calculated from marriage dates

JOHN HACKER
Abt 1550 -1616

John Hacker was born in Yeovil, Somerset, about 1550-55. during the reign of either Edward VI (1547-1553) or Mary I (1553-1558). This is an estimation taken from most accounts of Hacker genealogy. John was the forefather of the Nottinghamshire Hackers who were prominent in the area for many generations. He rose to be a 'gentleman of means', and his wealth derived from his employment as a solicitor and 'man of business', serving such members of the nobility as Bess of Hardwick and the 7th Earl of Shrewsbury.

Listed in the University of Oxford Register Vol II Part III 1571-1612, is *John Hacker suppl. B.C.L 31 October 1576.* That is he was given leave to supplicate, meaning he completed a degree in civil law.

Documents have survived that place John in Nottinghamshire and Derbyshire as early as 1584 and name him as *John of Hardwyke.* He also acquired land and property in other areas of Nottinghamshire such as Lowdham, Colston Bassett and Trowell.

In 1591, John purchased Sir Robert Sheffield's estate, which included the hall and lands in East Bridgford, Nottinghamshire, having been strategically placed there by the Earl of Shrewsbury, to wield influence.

John was knighted on 23 July 1603, dubbed at Whitehall as a Knight Bachelor.

On 28 November 1611, John was presented with his armorial bearings by Richard St George, Norroy and are described as *Arms, Azure, a cross vairé or and of the field between four mullets pierced of the second. Crest: On the trunk of a tree fessewise, a moorcock proper.*

HACKER CREST BY THE COLLEGE OF ARMS, REPRODUCED HERE BY KIND PERMISSION OF CHARLES MALCOLM-BROWN

John married Margaret Goode in the mid to late 1570s during the reign of Elizabeth I, and it is believed Margaret was the daughter of Thomas Goode, from Bassingbourn, Cambridgeshire. The only source found for this information is from *Some Account of the Hacker Family* by Major A E Lawson-Lowe (1941), a well-known Nottinghamshire historian at that time. Lowe's account is used as a reference by many researchers, but sadly, his own research sources cannot be located.

Nevertheless, there are clues lying elsewhere that can add weight to Margaret's birthplace and parentage. The will of Thomas Goode of Abington, Cambridgeshire, dated 1580, names a Margaret amongst his children. Although there is no baptism record for Margaret, her siblings are born during the 1560s and she appears to be one of the older children. Her birth during this time would fit well for her being of marrying age to John, albeit quite young. A full transcription of the will can be found in Appendix I. Abington is only a few miles from Bassingbourn, and the knowledge that in 1577 John Hacker presented a candidate for clergyman at East Hatley Church, also nearby - *Thomas Goode, a yeoman of Abington, presented his kinsman John Goode,* a connection can be placed between the two families.

A further clue connecting the families lies with Margaret's nephew, Edward Goode, to whom she bequeaths 22s in her will dated 1625. A full transcription of which can also be found in Appendix I.

Nicely settled in East Bridgford, John and Margaret raised their large family and socially engineered them into 'good' marriages. The exact order of their births can only be calculated from varying sources. No will for John Hacker can be found, but being a solicitor, he probably drew up a private settlement. On the other hand, Margaret in her will names her sons as Francis, *my eldest son,* followed by John, Rowland and Richard, *my youngest son.*

The daughters, however, are more complicated. Elizabeth is the only child to have a baptism record at East Bridgford. and this took place on 25 May 1593 at St Peter's. Her sister, Luce, had her first child in 1598, making her an older daughter. Marie married in 1617, possibly in her twenties, but with the lack of baptism records, these dates can only remain reasonable estimates.

John was buried at East Bridgford on 29 March 1616, followed by his wife, Margaret, on 6 January 1627. In her will, Margaret gives £10 (£2092 in 2022) towards the making of a tomb for herself and her deceased husband, and in St Peter's Church, East Bridgford, there is a magnificent wall monument depicting John and Margaret with four sons and two daughters. The inscription reads:

HERE LIETH BURIED YE BODIES OF JOHN HACKER OF BRIDGFORD ESQ. & MARGARET HIS WIFE, WHO LEFT ISSUES FOUR SONNES & 2 DAUGHTER, HEE DEPTED TS LIFE YE 28 MARCH A DMI 1620 & SHEE DEPTED TS LIFE YE 5 OF JANUARY 1627, IN WHOSE MEMORY THEIR SAID CHILDREN HAVE ERECTED TS MONUMENT

John's burial date is recorded incorrectly as 1620 not 1616, perhaps a slip of the stone mason's chisel...

The number of daughters depicted has been pondered over by historians. According to Margaret's will, there were actually three daughters still living, and mentioned in the following order, Elizabeth Harper, Mary Day, Luce Mayfield.

"Why one daughter is missing from the monument is unknown. It has been suggested she did not wish to contribute toward its making, but the real answer eludes us for now. Maybe further research will shed some light."

THE WALL MONUMENT AT EAST BRIDGFORD CHURCH
Image by Geoff Buxton - The Southwell and Nottingham Church History Project

THE SONS

FRANCIS - ELDEST SON

Francis's story will be told in the next chapter.

JOHN - SECOND SON

John was born about 1580 most probably in Somerset. The Hacker pedigree from the 1662 Visitation of Nottinghamshire (see page 77) informs us that John married Catherine Tevery and that they had six children. There is no record of their marriage, but it could have taken place about 1603-4 as their first child, William, was baptised on 3 July 1605 at St Helen's, Trowell, Nottinghamshire. He was followed by John on 2 January 1606, who must have died young as a second John was baptised in February 1608, then Thomas about 1609, George on 5 September 1611, Ann on 30 January 1612 and Rowland on 21 July 1616.

Catherine died before her husband, and he married a second time to Margaret Warbourton of Shelton, a widow, the licence was granted on 13 December 1623. When Margaret died in 1644, she was living in Nottingham and her will informs us that she was a widow. John was still alive in 1625 as he received £100 (*£20,920 in 2022*) from his mother's will. However, no burial record can be found at Trowell that fits for John, but it can be estimated that he died sometime between 1625 and 1644. In the will she mentions her *loving sons-in-law* William, George and Rowland, meaning her stepsons.

Trowell Hall was the family home, and Lawson Lowe, in his account of the Hacker family, quotes that the last John Hacker *removed to Trowell, and breaking his neck by an accidental fall down the staircase at the old manor house there.*

It would appear that accidents ran in the family...

In a letter *(Nottingham University Manuscripts & Special Collections MiE4/26)* from Edward Dovey to Francis Willoughby dated 18 October 1683, he writes that:

Mr Hacker who owned one third of the Manor of Trowell had died as a result of an accident; suggest that family should buy this property to consolidate Trowell estate.

The William mentioned above as a *loving son-in-law*, was buried on 10 October 1683 at Trowell, so this does imply that it was he who had the accident. He was the grandfather of John who broke his neck.

It has been extremely difficult to confirm many of these events due to missing records in the parish registers, and some confusion arose relating to the marriage of John and Catherine's daughter, Anne. The Visitation (see page 77) records her as marrying Nicholas Clarke, rector of Trowell. He was ordained in 1644 and became the rector at Trowell from about 1650. No marriage record can be found for the couple, but their daughter, Dorothy, was baptised at St Helen's, Trowell, on 11 September 1652, and then sadly, there is a burial for Anne on 12 September 1654. Nicholas married for a second time to Anne Westerbye on 23 December 1655.

Bearing all of this in mind, there is the matter of a marriage licence to be considered that was granted on 10 December 1634, between Anna Hacker of Trowell and Ferdinand Fitzrandolph of Kirkby-in-Ashfield.

The same page of the Visitation records this marriage as taking place between Anne, a daughter of John and Margaret of East Bridgford, but the marriage licence surely would have said Anne of East Bridgford, not Trowell. Furthermore, no Anne is mentioned in Margaret Hacker's will and if she had existed, it would mean a second daughter was missed off the wall monument. The conclusion drawn is that the licence must have been granted to John and Catherine's daughter, Anne. Yet, the marriage is not recorded in the St Wilfred's, Kirkby-in-Ashfield parish register. So, the question is, why did the marriage not take place? Further research into the Fitzrandolph family revealed a fascinating and tragic story and a possible explanation.

The wonderfully informative Archdeaconry Court Records revealed Ferdinand was presented several times between 1631-1642 for not receiving communion. So what was going on?

The Fitzrandolphs lived at Langton Hall, Kirkby-in-Ashfield, and they were a well-established family in the area. However, on the website *nottshistory.org.uk* there is talk of family arguments and about James of Langton Hall, who *had fallen upon evil times, and we can hardly imagine the sorrow that James and his wife had to encounter.* James was Ferdinand's father.

Perhaps under these circumstances, the Hackers thought it unwise for Anne to marry into such an unstable family, or maybe Ferdinand changed his mind at the last minute. It is unlikely we will ever know the true story. But in the Archdeaconry Court Records, further evidence can be found connected to this turbulent Fitzrandolph family. On 13 May 1630, James was presented to the court *for detayninge of a bell which did belong to the church and for a bible that did belong to the church*. The case was adjourned. Later, James was excommunicated on 29th May and absolved on 19th June. James died in 1636, and evidently, the family died out under tragic circumstances.

An inquisition dated 1638, in the *Index of Inquisitions Volume IV Charles I and later,* adds weight to the family dramas. The court was to decide whether Ferdinand was a lunatic or not. The original document is in Latin, and a translation was kindly carried out by expert Peter Foden, archivist, palaeographer and historian.

Document (WARD 7/90/199) at the National Archives.

The translation is as follows:

Ferdinand Fitzrandolfe Lunatic Nottingham *Examined by Hoskins Indented* **Inquisition** *held at Mansfield in Sherwood in the said County on the fifth day of January in the thirteenth year of the reign of our Lord Charles by the grace of God King of England Scotland France and Ireland Defender of the Faith etcetera before Matthew Palmer knight Robert Sutton Esquire and John Reynoldes Esquire the Escheator of the same County by virtue of a Commission of the said Lord the King, concerning Lunacy to be proved, to inquire whether Ferdinand Fitzrandolfe is a lunatic, or enjoys lucid intervals, so that he is not sufficient for his management of his lands, tenements and chattels, and concerning other questions specified in the said Commission, directed to six, five, four, or three of the same Commissioners and attached to this Inquisition, under oath, etcetera,* **Who, having been sworn,** *and charged, say upon their said oath, upon inspection and personal examination of the said Ferdinand Fitzrandolfe, before the Jurors aforesaid, that the said Ferdinand Fitzrandolfe named in the said Commission, at the time of holding this Inquisition, is, and, for the space of one year now last past and more, was in good and healthy memory and not a lunatic, nor does he [only] enjoy lucid intervals, and that he is well sufficient for his management of lands, tenements and chattels. In witness of which, etcetera.*

Peter summed up the document thus:

The Inquest is pretty emphatic isn't it? There must be a good story behind it. We would now talk about 'having capacity' but the Latin verb is 'sufficit'. If the Commissioners found him incapable, his land and other property would have been taken into the management of the Escheator until he recovered or his heir inherited, so it would have stopped him doing anything with his property (for example selling or giving it away) so perhaps that was what family members were trying to achieve.

Ferdinand's father had died in 1636, and two years later the inquest into Ferdinand's state of mind is being examined. Perhaps other family members disputed his right to Langton Hall, or were conniving to gain control of the estate. All intriguing scenarios.

An Admon. from the Deanery of Newark Administration Act Book reads: *Ferdinand Fitzrandolph, late of Langton Hall, co. Nottingham. Commission granted 8 May 1649 to Fitzrandolph Davenport of Sutton-in-Ashfield, co. Nottingham, gentleman)*

Ferdinand died without issue, but he had a sister, Isabel, who married Edward Davenport, with whom she had a son, Edward and a daughter, Isabel, and it is they who inherited Langton Hall and the possessions of the elder line of the Fitzrandolphs.

Perhaps they finally achieved what they set out to do.

ROWLAND - THIRD SON

Rowland was born about 1582-1584. Probably in Somerset, but documents at the Nottinghamshire Archives date his father in the area in 1584, so there is a chance he was born in Nottinghamshire. He married his first wife, Barbara Poole, at Barrowby, Lincolnshire on 5 September 1603, possibly aged between eighteen to twenty-one. There is some suggestion from other researchers that Rowland had married Barbara Jackson, the sister of Michael Jackson, a yeoman from East Bridgford. Indeed, in his will dated 1632, Michael mentions *my brother Hacker*, however, looking closer, Michael married Frances Poole of Syerston, Nottinghamshire, in 1594, which makes her highly likely to be Barbara Poole's sister, thus Rowland and Michael were brothers-in-law. The connection between Syerston and Barrowby is unclear, and unfortunately, due to the early years of their births, no baptisms can be found for either of them. Nevertheless, the two villages are only about fourteen miles apart.

Rowland and Barbara had three children together, and all were baptised at St Mary the Virgin, Lowdham. John on 29 May 1604, Margaret on 2 June 1609 and Mary on 17 January 1612. Sadly, John and Mary died within a few weeks of birth, and the family moved back to East Bridgford at some point.

At the age of around sixteen, the surviving daughter, Margaret, married Roger Waldron on 1 July 1624, by licence, at Colston Bassett, and they had about twelve children.

In Rowland's will, dated 1639, he bequeaths one of her children, Roger, his silver salter and best silver bowl, one fowling piece and a birding piece. None of the other grandchildren are beneficiaries.

THOMAS
SOUTHWELL
1631-1670
HOLDING A
FOWLING PIECE

Barbara was buried at East Bridgford on 15 June 1635. A few months later, a licence was granted on 6 February 1635/6 for Rowland to marry Elizabeth Yarborough, a widow, at St Mary's, Staining, London. Rowland gives his age as fifty or thereabouts, and Elizabeth gives hers as forty-three or thereabouts. Confirmation of the marriage is not possible, as the parish record is missing.

London seems a long distance from sleepy East Bridgford, and in the early 17th century the journey would have been lengthy and arduous. The mode of transport would either be on horseback or by long-covered wagons, usually transporting goods from city to city. The wealthy might have their own coach, and perhaps the Hackers owned one. Despite the difficulties, travel at home and abroad was more readily available than we possibly imagine, whether for pleasure or business by the rich or for undertaking a religious pilgrimage.

Stagecoaches first appeared in the 1630s and initially only covered the shorter distances linking nearby towns. By the later 1650s, there were a few longer routes between London and York and London and Exeter that coaches served, but in the summer months only. The trip from London to Exeter in 1658 took four days, and such travel had the advantage of accommodation in coaching inns along the way and advertised departure times. The chief problem, from the point of view of the poor, was the cost, with fares for inside passengers being typically 4d or 5d *(£2.73 and £3.37 in 2022)* a mile and for outside passengers 2d or 3d *(£1.29 or 2.09 in 2022)*. Today, London to Exeter is 178 miles, so calculating the total fare in 1658 ranged from £599.86 to £485.94 in today's money.

Rowland died in 1639 and was buried on 16 April at East Bridgford. In his will, he gives generously to the poor of East Bridgford and provides money for apprenticeships for poor children. He even bequeaths William Boscastle *in satisfaction of all the wrongs and trespasses done unto him,* a piece of meadow in Car Colston. It does make you ponder over what happened there.

Rowland also says he wishes to be buried in the north aisle of East Bridgford church, near his *deceased former wife.* He makes no mention of a wife named Elizabeth in his will, and attempts to track her down have been unsuccessful. So, whether the deceased former wife was Barbara or Elizabeth, is uncertain. Another mystery…

Rowland also received £100 from his mother's will.

RICHARD - FOURTH SON

On Richard's wall monument in St Augustine's, Flintham, Nottinghamshire, the inscription reads that he was born in 1586 at Hardwick. Document DDP 15/27 at the Nottinghamshire Archives, dated 1584, mentions his father, John Hacker of Hardewyke, gent., in the legal dealings taking place, so this would substantiate his birthplace claim.

WALL MONUMENT
ST AUGUSTINE'S

Richard married three times, and his first wife was Alice Hill of Sawley, Derbyshire, whom he wed in about 1607. The Visitation pedigree records he had the following children, John, born about 1609, followed by William, Francis, Elizabeth, Anne and Catherine. Richard's second wife was Catherine Ballard, formerly Stanford, whom he wed by licence in 1619, and name association suggests she could have been Catherine's mother. Sadly, his wife, Catherine, died only a year after their marriage. She was buried on 19 October 1620, Wymeswold, Leicestershire. *Some Account of the Hacker Family* by Major A E Lawson-Lowe, mentions another son Edward, however, his name is not recorded in the Visitation.

Not to be deterred, Richard married for a third time to Anne Wood on 28 November 1644, at Flintham, where the family lived in the hall. By now, he was about fifty-eight years of age and being a gentleman of wealth and good standing, he was appointed High Sheriff of Nottingham in 1646. He died eight years later in 1654 and is buried at Flintham.

He also received £100 (*£20,920 in 2022*) from his mother's will.

SONS OF SONS

Two of Richard's sons deserve a well-earned mention in this narrative. Born in the early 1600s, William and Francis both became wealthy merchants residing in London. William is recorded in Boyd's Inhabitants of London and Family Units 1200-1946 as a merchant and citizen who married Martha Smith. This record also reveals William's untimely death, which came about in Germany, where he was murdered on 26 March 1651 and buried in Frankfurt. So, what was happening in the world that could have got him murdered?

1651 was during the Commonwealth Period of England following the brutal Civil Wars, and the beheading of Charles I. England was declared a republic, and it was a time of tremendous change. Germany was also emerging from the Thirty Years War, another bloody and devasting period of history. Was William in Frankfurt on business, or is there another theory?

Espionage in the 17th century was widespread, and many spies were actually female. Perhaps William's occupation provided him with an excellent cover to undertake spying missions, but he was discovered on his final mission and assassinated. On the other hand, he could just as well have been in the wrong place at the wrong time, poor chap.

His brother, Francis, has an interesting history. He was incredibly wealthy, and alongside his main dealings as a Salter, part of his wealth was derived from tobacco in Virginia, USA. Shipping records place him in 1639 and 1672 importing tobacco, a lucrative business in the 17th century and sadly, one that also involved slavery.

Francis died in 1683 and left one of the most detailed wills I have encountered, which indicates the vastness of his wealth and lists numerous possessions and to whom he bequeaths them. I found item seven most intriguing and emphasises the sad fact that everything a woman owned belonged to her husband in that period of history and was so until the Married Woman's Property Act of 1870:

Item 7: I give my wife her clossett with all things belonging to it silver and pewter neither intended as to belong to her closet

She also receives a Persian carpet, two Spanish tables and leather carpets. His daughter Lucy is also given a Spanish table, a Turkish carpet and £1500 (£253,200 in 2022). These are just a few of the extremely expensive items listed, and the full transcript can be found in Appendix I.

THE DAUGHTERS

Fortunately, Margaret named her daughters by their married names in her will, and despite there being a gap in the East Bridgford baptism records between 1599 and 1613, the fact they begin as early as 1557, left a breadcrumb trail of clues, enough to piece together something about each of them. The order in which they are named is calculated from the known dates of a few marriages and baptisms.

LUCE (LUCY)

My daughter Luce Meafield', as it is written in Margaret's will, was possibly born between 1576-79, probably in Somerset, and she married William Mayfield in about 1597. Their first child, Helen, was baptised at St Peter's, East Bridgford on 19 July 1598. Due to the gap in the register, we are prevented from knowing if any children were born before John, who was baptised on 3 September 1615. Next came Anne on 28 September 1617, Gabriel on 8 August 1619, Luce on 29 September 1622 and Thomas on 8 August 1628.

From her mother, Luce inherits £20 (£4184 in 2022), a gold ring worth 3 guineas (£659) and a share of the diamonds that Margaret *bought off her son Francis.* Luce's son, John, receives £5 (£1046), her daughter Luce 40s (£418.40) and her other children also receive 40s a piece.

Luce was buried at East Bridgford on 3 June 1637, as Lucia, wife of William.

MARIE (MARY)

Marie was possibly born about 1589-1590, probably in Somerset. A marriage licence was granted on 19 June 1617, at Wysall, Nottinghamshire, to Marie Hacker and John Day, a merchant of the City of London. So, on paper, it looks as if Marie also married well.

If the couple resided in London after their marriage, there is a selection of baptisms for children of a John and Mary Day and also burials of Mary Day, but without any further clues, it is impossible to be sure if any of them are the records required.

Marie inherited £30 (£6276 in 2022) from her mother along with her share of the diamonds and what would have been a treasured item, her gold poesie ring. Quite possibly a betrothal ring from her husband, John.

THE LANGAR POESY RING
c16th century
The inscription reads
AMOR VINCIT - 'Love Conquers'

A poesy (or posie, posy) is a short verse, often from a poem, inscribed on a ring. Poesy rings were first commonly worn in the 15th century, and they remained popular throughout the 17th century. They initially featured words inscribed on the outside of the bands, but from the 16th century, the words began to be inscribed on the inside of the rings. Most Poesy rings were made of gold, but there are silver examples decorated with gilding. An early manuscript of poetry written during the 16th century included over one hundred Poesy ring inscriptions.

ELIZABETH

Elizabeth was baptised on 25 May 1593, at East Bridgford. She married twice, first to Thomas Wightman by licence on 9 January 1614, making her twenty-one years of age when she married.

THOMAS WIGHTEMAN, & Elizabeth Hacker, d. of John Hacker of East Bridgford, esq.; at same

---

Sadly, this was a short-lived marriage as Thomas died just over a year after they wed. He was buried on 5 February 1615, at East Bridgford. Whether he lived to witness the birth of his son, John, is unknown due to the gap in the register.

Her second marriage appears to be one of significance in the bringing together of two prominent families. Richard Harpur of Littleover, Derbyshire was her second spouse, the son of Sir Richard Harpur. They married about 1616, very soon after the death of her first husband. Their home in Littleover is recorded as having ten hearths in the 1674 Hearth Tax Returns, which is a substantial dwelling according to the table below of gentry and nobility status.

The Hearth Tax was introduced in 1662, and records exist for most counties for the years 1664 and 1674.

Each liable householder was to pay one shilling, twice a year, for each fire, hearth and stove in each dwelling or house. The lists comprise the names of the head of the household or the property owner and include those exempt, that is, those too poor to contribute to poor and church rates, or whose property was worth less than 20 shillings a year. The table is only a guide, and the Hacker's home in East Bridgford had seven hearths, placing the two families on a very similar social level.

Elizabeth and Richard had eight known children, Richard, John, Henry, Joseph, William, Elizabeth, Mary and Catherine.

Elizabeth also inherits from her mother's will. Her son, John Wightman, receives £20 (£4184 in 2022), and the rest of her children with Richard Harpur, four score pounds [£80] (£16,740 in 2022) divided between them. Elizabeth is also given her mother's largest gold ring and her share of the diamonds.

So far, a burial record for Elizabeth has not been located.

OTHER BENEFICIARIES

Margaret Hacker's will is a wonderfully detailed list of her personal possessions that she wishes to be kept in the family. She gives generously to her children and also ensures her daughters-in-law receive gifts.

Francis's wife, Margaret, and Rowland's wife, Barbara, are given a *piece of gold of the value of 21 shillings (£219.70 in 2022)*. Barbara also receives a gold ring worth four guineas (£878.70 in 2022).

Numerous grandchildren receive £5 (£1046 in 2022) and her step-granddaughter, Elizabeth Rossell, is bequeathed a cupboard with a press, which was an early form of clothes wardrobe. Furniture, linens, silverware, cutlery etc, were valuable items and often itemised in wills to be passed on to future generations.

In 2022, the value of the money and jewellery Margaret bequeaths is at least £138,000, and that does not include the diamonds, the linen press and other items. A full transcription of Margaret's will can be found in Appendix I.

No of Hearths	Social Status of Occupier
1	Labourers and the poorer sort of husbandmen
2-3	Craftsmen, tradesmen. yeomen
4-7	Wealthier craftsmen, tradesman and yeomen, merchants
8+	Gentry and Nobility

WHAT'S FOR DINNER TONIGHT?

To sowce a Pike, Carpe, or Breame.

Draw your fish, but scale it not: save the Liver and the refuse of it, slit the said refuse, and wash it. Then take a pottle of fayre water, a quart of white Wine, and a fagot of sweet Hearbes: so soone as you see your wine boyle, throw in your Fish with the scales on, and when you see your Fish boyle, poure in a little Vinegar, and it will make your Fish crispe. Then take up your Fish, and put it in a Tray. Then put into the liquour some whole Pepper, a little whole Ginger, and when it is boyled together well with a little Salt, and colde, put in your Fish into an earthen Panne: when you serve it in, serve Gelly in Sawcers, with a little fine Ginger about the Sawcers sides, and Fennell on your Fish.

Taken from A New Booke of Cookerie, 1615

COST OF LIVING

Privy Council Star Chamber records from James I's reign include the following expenses
1558-1603

1½ fresh salmon	38s
2 pheasant	20s
12 quail	18s
18 rabbits	16s
1½ lambs	15s
Conger eel	14s 4d
Six plaice	9s

THE ARCHDEACON PRESENTS...

Not all was well in East Bridgford. There be womanising and too much idle chatter at church among the usual village activities.

Crime and punishment in the 16th-17th centuries was taken care of by the church courts. The Archdeacon was charged with overseeing the spiritual and moral well-being of the parishioners in his archdeaconry and upholding canon law. People were brought before the courts for a wide variety of offences, including religious dissent, non-payment of church dues, sexual misconduct, clandestine marriages, disorderly behaviour in church precincts, and superstitious practices.

On 12 May 1623, the rector of St Peter's presented the following persons at the Archdeacons Court:

Wm Jacson, late churchwarden of the parish, deferred his accounts longer than the time appointed by the canon and then passed them without the consent or presence of the rector.

Wm Houmes, churchwarden for the last year, brought wine to the communion table on Easter day that was 'full of filthie and sluttish dregs'.

Henrie Ragsdale, son of Wm Ragsdale, gave forth words and brags that he has lain with 'three sundrie kinds of women'.

There is never a fair Bible in the church, of the new translation, the one that is there is torn and is missing some pages.

John Jacson and Arthur Redgate, parishioners, for sitting irreverently in time of divine service with their hats on their heads etc., John Jacson in the time of the reading of the Gospel and Arthur Redgate during the singing of the psalm, both on 25 March 1632.

The parishioners spend more time gazing and talking in the churchyard after the minister is in his seat and will not come into the church at the first warning; the churchwardens are negligent in presenting them.

The parish is so great that the churchwardens often stand in need of sidesmen or assistants, humbly craving that two neighbours might be appointed for that purpose.

There are many holes over the windows and under the leads of the church, so that doves and daws [jackdaws] huddle and creep through them into the church, to the fouling and annoyance of the church and the interruption of divine service.

There are two chests wanting three locks, one to keep the register in, the other for alms given to the poor.

Ellen Spurre, Henrie Kerke, Elizabeth Burrowes and Isabell Samet for sitting idly at the church door upon the stone bench after the minister came into his seat and prayed for the preparation of the service.

Mrs Wartnibee, widow, and goodwife Ragsdale, wife of Wm Ragsdale for standing and talking idily at the church porch in time of divine service

Wm Jacson has one or two books concerning the church accounts and keeps them in his custody, refusing to deliver them to the minister or the churchwardens.

So, once caught and found guilty, what was their punishment?

> **"Humiliation in front of the entire church congregation came first. The person would be made to stand on a chair, bare-legged and bare-headed, wearing a white robe and forced to confess their sins to all present and vow never to do it again. Did this work? Repeat offenders are often noted, but then they also are today."**

WITCHES

There was much superstition and ignorance in 17th-century England, and the witch hunt was at its most intense stage during the Civil War and the Puritan era of the mid-17th century.

Witchcraft had been illegal since 1563, and hundreds of women were wrongly accused and punished. 'Proof' of being a witch could be a third nipple, an unusual scar or birthmark, a boil, a growth, or even owning a cat or other pet (a witch's familiar or evil spirit). Confessions were often made under torture, and suspects suffered Ordeal by Water. There are different descriptions of the process, but basically, the suspect was lowered into water by a rope. If they sank, they were considered innocent, whereas if they floated, this indicated witchcraft. After a show trial, the victim was executed usually by hanging, although in Scotland, the bodies were burned after the poor victim had been strangled.

An intriguing entry in the East Bridgford parish register suggests the possibility of witchcraft afoot in the village during 1637. At the start of the 1637 burials, the rector had written *pestis invaluit* 'plague is becoming strong', and tragically there were eighty-nine burial entries for that year, including Richard Kerke, a *nonagenarian*.

Then, on 12 November 1637, Anna Key was buried following *que aquis immersa et inventa*, translated to 'immersed in water and found out.' Was poor Anna believed to be a witch and subject to the terrifying water ordeal?

Even more suspicious is that the entry in the parish register is crossed out, perhaps in an attempt to obliterate her from the records.

WOODCUT ON A PRINTED PAMPHLET AVAILABLE FOR PURCHASE IN 1643

"**Did she die from drowning during her ordeal, or was she hanged? I doubt we will ever know. Nor what led her to be suspected of witchcraft in the first place. Perhaps her only crime was attempting to help sufferers of the 'plague' which hit the village that year.**"

Francis Hacker I Full name of Husband	About 1576, Somerset Birth Date and Place
John Hacker His Father	About 1597 Marriage Date and Place
Margaret His Mother with Maiden Name	20 Jan 1646 St Peter's, East Bridgford VESPERI at night Burial Date and Place
Anne Full name of Wife	About 1576 Birth Date and Place
Unknown Her Father	
Unknown Her Mother with Maiden Name	Oct 1616 St Mary's the Virgin, Lowdham Burial Date and Place

And The Children Were.............................

1. John	Born: abt 1598	Married: Susan Clud 8 Oct 1620 Halam	Buried: 3 Dec 1632 Lowdham
2. Richard	Born: abt 1599-1600	Married: Unknown	Died: Unknown
3. Margaret	Bapt: 1 Apr 1602 Gedling		Died: ?young
4. Elizabeth	Born: abt 1603-4	Married: Gervase Rossell (her step-brother) licence 16 Jan 1621	Died: 1633
5. Francis II The Regicide	Bapt: 16 Mar 1605 Gedling	Married: Isabel Brunts 5 July 1632 St Peter's Nottm by licence	Died: 19 Oct 1660 Tyburn Gallows, London
6. Thomas	Born: abt 1606-7	Married: probably unmarried	Buried: 12 May 1643 East Bridgford Occisus in Colston Bassett
7. Katherine	Bapt: 5 May 1608 St Mary's Nottm		Buried: 24 May 1608 St Mary's Nottm
8. Jane	Bapt: 23 Apr 1609 St Mary's Nottm	Married: William Townes 22 Oct 1638 Colston Bassett	Died: Unknown
9. Rowland	Bapt: 8 Jan 1610 Lowdham	Married: Unknown	Buried: 7 Oct 1674 East Bridgford
10. Anne	Born: abt 1611	Married: Unknown	Buried: ?18 Aug 1650 East Bridgford (a) Mason
11. Alice	Bapt: 17 Jan 1612 Lowdham	Married: John Grocock	Buried: 2 Oct 1673 Lowdham
12. Marie	Born: unk		Buried: July 1616 Lowdham
13. Peter	Bapt: 15 Mar 1615 Lowdham		Buried: Sep 1616 Lowdham

FRANCIS HACKER I
Abt 1576 -1646

Francis was born about 1576, most likely in Somerset, the eldest son of John Hacker and Margaret Goode, during the reign of Elizabeth I. This period of history is often called the Golden Age, a time when England experienced peace and prosperity, the arts flourished, and so did the Hacker family. Francis continued as agent to the nobility, such as the Earl of Rutland, and he married Anne probably in the late 1590s. Unfortunately, no record of their marriage has survived, however, baptisms for some of their children have, and they took place in Lowdham, Gedling and Nottingham. These baptism records support their union, which produced at least twelve sons and daughters, who it can be assumed were all born in Nottinghamshire.

The existence of their eldest son was confirmed in an Archdeaconry Court record dated 1608, which mentions Francis and Anne Hacker and their son, John. Also, Francis's will contains extremely useful information regarding his offspring.

Out of their twelve, possibly thirteen children, sadly, four or five of them died as infants and to make matters worse, their mother, Anne, was buried at St Mary the Virgin, Lowdham in October 1616, only one month after the last child, Peter, was buried in September 1616. Perhaps her luck in surviving childbirth ran out, or maybe plague or another disease took Anne and her infants away.

With numerous young children to care for, Francis married for a second time just over a year after Anne's death, to a widow, Margaret Rossell née

17TH-CENTURY FAMILY 1640s
By William Dobson

Whalley, the daughter of Walter Whalley, gentleman of Cotgrave. They wed on 23 December 1617 at East Bridgford. Possibly nine of his children with Anne were still living, and the eldest, John, would have been about eighteen years old when his father remarried, closely followed by his brother, Richard. Both of these brothers have their own tales to tell.

Margaret brought three young children with her from her first marriage in 1605 to George Rossell of Radcliffe-on-Trent. They were Gervase, George and Elizabeth (*1614 Visitation of Nottinghamshire.*) No further information pertaining to George can be found, as for his two siblings… more on them later.

Francis Hacker I Full name of Husband	About 1576 Birth Date and Place
John Hacker His Father	23 December 1617 East Bridgford Marriage Date and Place
Margaret His Mother with Maiden Name	20 Jan 1646 St Peter's, East Bridgford Burial Date and Place
Margaret Rossell née Whalley Full name of Wife	About 1584-7 Birth Date and Place
Walter Whalley Her Father	27 November 1634 St Peter's, East Bridgford Burial Date and Place

An interesting connection here is that by marriage through the Whalley family, Margaret was the great, great-niece of Oliver Cromwell's aunt.

A confusing burial for Elizabeth, the wife of Francis, was recorded at East Bridgford on 27 November 1634. Theoretically, Margaret may have died and Francis took a third wife, but there are no records to substantiate this. So, the question asked is, did the vicar transcribe her name wrongly and it was actually Margaret?

The burial of a Barbara Hacker, the daughter of Francis, at East Bridgford, on 4 January 1635, also caused some confusion. Who was this Barbara? There is no baptism entry for her at East Bridgford, nor can one be found elsewhere. It is feasible age-wise that Margaret, or a third wife, could have conceived a child with Francis, however, with no records to corroborate Barbara's parentage, this remains a question yet unanswered.

Although the Hacker family members are buried at East Bridgford, many of them under the church, from 1625 onwards, Francis, Margaret and his large family lived in Colston Bassett. *A History of Colston Bassett, Thoroton Society Record Series Vol. IX (1942)* tells us that Francis had a house built on land he had purchased there. In 1628, he inherited £300 *(£62,760 in 2022)* from his mother, Margaret, quite a sizeable amount to put towards the building of his new home, perhaps?

A survey of Francis's estate in Colston Bassett in 1662 describes the house, and it gives a wonderful insight into how people lived in the 17th century.

The *Faire Dwelling house,* known as the Hall House, consists of a cellar, a ground floor, comprising of one hall, a kitchen, a small room by the hall, the buttery, a wainscoted parlour with another little fore room within and a small closet. The first floor has many handsome rooms and garrets (habitable attics) above. Outside there is a four-acre garden, an orchard, a tiled barn, a tiled malthouse, a stable and an old thatched brewery.

The house is still standing today (2024) and is now called the Manor Farm House.

Francis lived a further twelve years at Colston Bassett before he passed away and was buried at East Bridgford on 20 January 1646. The entry reads he was buried 'Vesperi', meaning at night. Why? A most intriguing thought to ponder over.

The grandiose funerals of the elite had previously tended to take place during daylight hours, but during the 17th century, nighttime burials were increasingly preferred amongst the English nobility. That Francis chose to be buried at night does suggest he was a devoutly religious and pious man. It was also a time in history when everyone's faith was being tested to its limit.

THE HOUSE AT COLSTON BASSETT IN 2023

THE SONS

JOHN - ELDEST SON

John was born about 1598. He married Susan Clud on 8 October 1620, at St Michael's, Halam, Nottinghamshire. Susan's father was Thomas Clud of Arnold, and their pedigree in the 1662 Visitation is entered as Clud of Southwell. As the eldest son, John would surely have been required to take on certain responsibilities in the family business that involved him travelling around the county. Arduous journeys on horseback, no doubt, and the necessity for some creature comforts on arrival at his various destinations.

Discovered in the records of the Archdeaconry Court dated 1622 was a certain John Hacker of Lowdham: *There is a public fame that one John Hacker of Lowdham lives in shameful adultery with one Mary Slack, whom he maintains one while at Chesterfield, another while at Mannsfeild and another while at Nicholas Hancock's house called 'the pittance', in so much that the said Hacker's wife has twice come to Mansfield to seek her husband and fetch him home from the said 'common, noted and reputed whore';*

Scandalous!

He was buried at Lowdham on 3 December 1632 as John Hacker of Gunthorpe, gent. He would only have been in his early thirties when he died. Under what circumstances is unknown!

RICHARD - SECOND SON

Richard was born about 1599-1600, and no marriage or burial can be found for him. Although not unusual for that period of time, what we do have is an intriguing passage found in his father Francis's will, dated 1640, by which time his eldest son, John, was dead.

Whereas I have a sonn called Richard my oldest sonn whom I knowe not whether hee bee living or dead but being minded to dispose of my Lande Tenemente and hereditaments from him in Case hee should bee living I doo therefore hereby bequeath and give unto my Sonn Francis Hacker All that my house Lande Tenemente in Colston Bassett.... Etc

What family troubles caused Richard to disappear must have been serious. Historians have described Richard as a *ne'er do well* and that being the reason for him being disinherited, but there have to be numerous others, and the real reason will probably remain unknown.

FRANCIS - THIRD SON

Francis, the parliamentarian and regicide, will be discussed in the next chapter.

THOMAS - FOURTH SON

No baptism for Thomas can be found, but he was probably born about 1606-7. It is difficult to say whether he married or not and after an extensive search, no records have come to light. His life was tragically cut short when he was killed in May 1643 during a Civil War skirmish at Colston Bassett, Nottinghamshire. He was buried at East Bridgford on 12 May 1643. Written next to his burial record are the words *Occisus* [killed] *at Colston Bassett.*

This brutal Civil War ripped families apart, with sons, brothers and fathers taking opposing sides, and such was the case in the Hacker family. Thomas and his younger brother, Rowland, were loyal to the king, unlike their older brother, Francis, who took up Oliver Cromwell's cause. Thomas was set to inherit the Colston Bassett estate on his father's death, but pre-deceased him, and because the will was never changed following Thomas's death, this caused serious repercussions after the Civil War ended. More on that later.

ROWLAND - FIFTH SON

Rowland is rather a mysterious chap and is also deserving of his own chapter in this book.

PETER - SIXTH SON

Peter's life was brief. He was baptised at Lowdham on 15 March 1615 and buried in September 1616.

THE DAUGHTERS

Even though most of the girls have birthdates except for Elizabeth, Anne and Marie, once again, placing them in order of their births was quite challenging.

MARGARET - POSSIBLY THE FIRST DAUGHTER

Baptised on 1 April 1602 at All Hallow's, Gedling, nothing more is known about Margaret. She is not mentioned in her father's will, so presumably, she died young. It is quite sad when nothing else can be found about a person's life.

ELIZABETH - POSSIBLY THE SECOND DAUGHTER

Elizabeth was probably born about 1603-1604. The relationship with her choice of husband required some clarification as to whether it was prohibited. Not only was he her step-brother, but fifteen or sixteen years old at the time, and Elizabeth about seventeen or eighteen.

The table of prohibited degrees printed at the end of the Book of Common Prayer, which lists members of the Anglican Church who are forbidden by Church Law to marry, is long and complicated. Many of them are obvious such as not marrying your father, mother, sister, brother etc. But then it becomes bizarre: a man may not marry his sister-in-law, despite not being blood relatives, or a non-blood grandchild or your brother's wife, after the brother has died, of course, amongst other non-blood relationships. With these kinds of prohibited marriages, one would suspect that a marriage between step-siblings would also be prohibited. However, if it is proved that they are not related by blood from the wider circle of the same lineage and thus from a different clan, then they can marry. Therefore, the wording on the marriage licence granted on 19 January 1621 for Elizabeth to marry her step-brother, Gervase Rossell, is perhaps an attempt to explain to the church that the couple were not blood relatives.

Gervase Rossell, of Radcliffe-on-Trent, gent, & Elizabeth Hacker, the natural and lawful daughter of Frauncis Hacker of same esq.; at same.

As Gervase's stepfather, Francis would have overseen the Rossell estate until Gervase became of age, and no doubt desired it to stay in the family, thus an arranged marriage between the two families would make this so.

The possibility that marriages such as Elizabeth's and even cousins may or may not have been frowned upon was explained by Professor Probert, author of Marriage Law for Genealogists:

'In terms of whether it would have been frowned upon, there doesn't seem to be any instinctive distaste for marriages between couples who have grown up together - after all, Austen's Mansfield Park ends with a marriage between cousins who have grown up in the same house with no sense that this is in any way odd.'

The 1662 Visitation records three children from the marriage, George, born about 1626, Thomas baptised on 4 November 1627, and Anne on 21 September 1628 at Radcliffe-on-Trent.

Elizabeth died in 1633, and Gervase re-married to Jane Ascough in 1640, but not before he fathered an illegitimate daughter with Abigale Smith. The child, Marie, was baptised on 19 August 1638 at Radcliffe-on-Trent.

During the English Civil War, Gervase served as captain in The King's army and was recorded as a defender in the Royalist garrison at Newark against the parliamentarians in 1643. He died about 1660.

KATHERINE - THIRD DAUGHTER

Poor Katherine's life ended within three weeks of her birth. She was baptised at St Mary's, Nottingham on 5 May 1608 and buried at the same just over two weeks later, on 24 May 1608. The move to Nottingham was probably connected to family business as the Hacker empire expanded.

JANE - FOURTH DAUGHTER

Jane was baptised on 23 April 1609 at St Mary's, Nottingham. She fared better than her sisters; survived childhood and married William Townes on 22 October 1638 at Colston Bassett.

Name associations on records are wonderful, and sometimes much can be gleaned from them. The bondsmen on this marriage licence are Francis, her brother and William, her cousin.

The couple lived in Ancaster after their marriage, and there is a baptism there for a daughter, Anne, in 1639. Unfortunately, nothing more can be found

WILLIAM TOWNES, of Sudbrooke, p. Ancaster, co. Linc., gent., & a bac., & Jane Hacker, of Colston Bassett, spr. [Bond by Francis Hacker, of Stathern, co. Leic., gent., & William Hacker, of Trowell, gent.]

regarding Jane at present. She possibly died before her father, Francis, wrote his will in 1640, as he does not mention her.

There is a William Townes who died at Sudbrooke in 1711/12 whose name is recorded in the Lincolnshire Inventory of the Goods of Deceased persons. This could possibly be their son.

ANNE - FIFTH DAUGHTER

No baptism for Anne can be found, but she is named first in her father's will and received a considerable legacy of £600 *(£90,730 in 2022)*. She was unmarried when he wrote his will in 1640, so this was a generous portion for her to take to a future marriage if a suitable husband came along. With regards to Anne, there is a matter that requires careful clarification regarding a suggested marriage to a Mr Marshall.

In Hubbard's essay, dated 1941, he quotes from *The Journal of George Fox* that in 1655 George Fox: *went into Leicestershire, where Colonell Hacker said he would imprison me againe. I came to Whetstone where his troopers had taken me before, and Colonell Hacker's wife and Marshall came to the meeting and was convinct (who remains a Friende to this day)*

Hubbard somehow concluded that it meant Francis's brother-in-law, Marshall, the husband of his sister, Anne. This is very perplexing as the printed transcript for this particular page clearly says:

> 222   JOURNAL OF GEORGE FOX   [1655
>
> So I went into Leicestershire where Colonel Hacker said if I come down there he would imprison me again, though Oliver Protector had set me at liberty; but I came down to Whetstone where his troopers had taken me before; and Colonel Hacker's wife[3] and his marshall came to the meeting and were convinced.
> [3] Isabel Hacker, formerly Brunts

The word marshall is found several times elsewhere in the journal, so it could be concluded that the marshall mentioned was just that, a marshall or a type of bodyguard.

There is an intriguing burial to consider at East Bridgford for Anna Hacker (a) Mason on 18 August 1650. Perhaps the (a) means alias, and Anna was married to a Mr Mason? This could have been to preserve the rights to her family inheritance. However, there are no other records to substantiate this possibility at present.

ALICE - SIXTH DAUGHTER

Alice was baptised on 17 January 1612 at Lowdham and married Mr Grocock, as she is named thus in her father's will. Again, no marriage record can be found, however, there are two baptisms at Lowdham for John Grocock on 23 April 1639 and Anne on 15 June 1640 whose father is recorded as John. So presumably, Alice married John.

Alice received £100 *(15,120 in 2022)* in her father's will. Unfortunately, no burial can be found for her.

MARIE - SEVENTH DAUGHTER

The only record to indicate Marie's life is her burial at Lowdham in July 1616. The quandary here is when was Marie born?

Her mother, Anne, died shortly after the birth of Peter, who was buried two months before Marie, therefore, she must have been older than him. There is a three-year gap between Peter and Alice in 1612-1615, where she might fit in. All food for thought.

THE ROSSELL STEP-CHILDREN

Elizabeth first married Nicholas Strelley Esq., with whom she had a son, George, and he was baptised on 28 August 1631 at All Saints, Strelley, Nottinghamshire. Nicholas died soon after the birth of his son and was buried on 30 September 1631.

Elizabeth married a second time to Sir Richard Byron, the second Lord Byron, with whom she had ten children, including William Byron the third Lord Byron. According to the Rossell pedigree in the 1662 Visitation, she died in about 1647. This is the Elizabeth who inherited the cupboard with the press from Margaret.

Gervase has already been discussed, it was he who married Elizabeth Hacker the *'natural and lawful daughter of Francis Hacker.'*

George seems to have disappeared from history; another victim of missing records.

THE STINKING RICH

The phrase 'the stinking rich' has many origins, one of which is related to the desire of prominent people in every village and town to be buried inside the church. They wished to be closer to God after their death, and this was often requested in their last will and testament.

That they wanted this, did not mean their wish was always granted. Nevertheless, a huge number of bodies do lie beneath church floors, and this became a decidedly smelly problem. Hence the origin of the phrase, as it was only the rich folk who could afford such burials. The vile stench of putrid corpses inside the churches became a serious dilemma, but it was not until the 1857 Burial Act that this stinky and unsanitary practice was abolished.

Some members of the Hacker family wished to be buried in the north aisle or quire of St Peter's, East Bridgford. Unfortunately, there are no stones on the church floor bearing their names, and neither is there a record of who is under the floor.

We do know that Margaret Hacker had expressed her wish to be buried in the north chapel at St Peter's, with John, and their monument is displayed on the north wall of the church. Francis's brother, Rowland, also wanted to be buried in the north aisle next to his wife, and Rowland II requested a place in the north quire. Even Francis, despite living in Colston Bassett, wanted to be buried in East Bridgford church next to his wife.

Hopefully, they were all granted their desires, and there is more on Hacker burials in Appendix III.

ST PETER'S CHURCH
EAST BRIDGFORD
2022

HACKER WALL
MONUMENT

CHURCH INTERIOR

Hacker Wall Monument

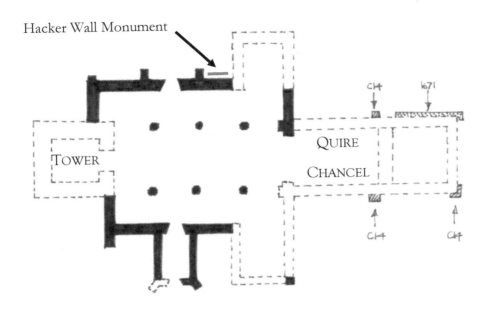

PLAN OF ST PETER'S CHURCH 1320-1340

Showing reconstruction of the 1320/1340 extension to nave (shaded parts still extant)

When Dr Robert Thoroton wrote his history of Nottinghamshire in 1677, he recorded that the church still had its stained glass windows, the transept tombs and the old tower and roof, but that the fabric was decaying. An extensive restoration was undertaken in the 1770s which entailed the removal of, and the rebuilding of the tower from the plinth upwards and the replacement of the nave roof. The transepts were completely removed and the aisle walls extended across their openings. Alarmingly, the altar tombs were thrown out into the graveyard. A new pulpit with a sounding board and enclosed pews were also acquired.

Image and information from Southwell and Nottingham Church History Project

Hacker Wall Monument

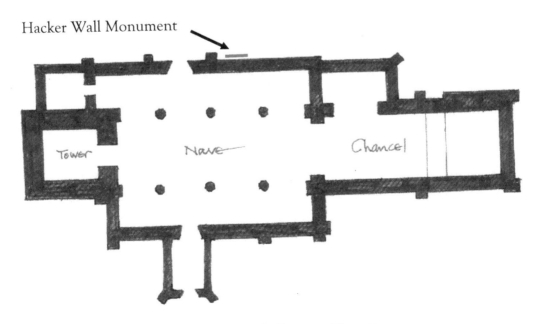

PLAN OF ST PETER'S CHURCH TODAY

Image courtesy of the Southwell and Nottingham Church History Project

Francis Hacker II Colonel & Regicide Full name of Husband	16 Mar 1605 All Hallows, Gedling Baptism Date and Place	
Francis Hacker His Father	5 Jul 1632 St Peter's Nottm Marriage Date and Place	
Anne His Mother with Maiden Name	19 Oct 1660 Tyburn Gallows Death Date and Place	

Isabel Brunts Full name of Wife	16 Jun 1613 St Peter & Paul's, Mansfield Baptism Date and Place
Gabriel Brunts Her Father	
Isabell Dand(e) Her Mother with Maiden Name	10 Dec 1677, Stathern, Leics Although it is thought she may have been buried in the Quaker graveyard at Long Clawson Burial Date and Place

And The Children Were.................................

1. Francis III Physician Extra LCRP	Bapt: 26 May 1633 Stathern	Married: Anne Wolfris 9 Feb 1672 St Botolph, London	Buried: 13 Mar 1693 St Antholin, London
2. Anne	Bapt: 25 Mar 1634 Stathern	Married: Unknown	Died: Unknown
3. Elizabeth	Bapt: 9 Oct 1637 Stathern	Married: Capt. Clement Needham Abt 1653	Buried: 2 Dec 1666 Rearsby, Lecis
4. Isabel	Bapt: 24 Jan 1638 Stathern		Buried: 30 Apr 1646 Stathern
5. Mary	Bapt: 8 Mar 1639 Stathern	Married: Unknown	Died: Unknown
6. Barbara	Bapt: 18 Jul 1641 Stathern		Buried: 29 Apr 1646 Stathern
7. Samuel Haberdasher	Born: Abt 1648	Married: [1]Elizabeth Byfield 8 Dec 1681 All Hallows, Staining [2]Elizabeth Coupe (widow of Henry Coupe) 4 Apr 1711 Allestree, Derbys	Buried: 20 Feb 1723 St Alkmunds, Duffield

FRANCIS HACKER II
1605 -1660

FRANCIS HACKER
This recently discovered portrait of Francis has emerged, and a full account of its provenance can be found in Appendix IV

Image reproduced by the kind permission of Charles Malcolm Brown

Francis was baptised on 16 March 1605 at All Hallows, Gedling, the third son of Francis and Anne. The monarch reigning at the time was James I of England, who also ruled as James VI of Scotland.

As Francis began his life journey, born into a wealthy and prestigious family, never could he have known as a young man that his life would end on the gallows at Tyburn, hanged as a traitor for his involvement in the execution of Charles I.

So, Francis was a respectable twenty-seven years old when he married Isabel Brunts on 5 July 1632 at St Peter's, <u>Nottingham</u>, and they made their home at Stathern, Leicestershire. All accounts say they lived in a hall situated at the side of Mill Hill. However, new research has been carried out, and it is now known that Francis had two properties. One was a freehold property with two acres of land, *his demesne,*

FRAUNCIS HACKER, jun., of Coston Bassett, gent., & Isabell Brunts, late of East Bridgford, but now of Bingham, spr.; at St Peter's

and most probably where he lived, the other was a leasehold property with eighty acres of land. It is possible that a farm of this size could have been a manor farm, and thus, the property is more likely to be a large house as opposed to a hall. This would be the house that stood on Mill Hill.

Francis and Isabel's first child, Francis, was born in 1633, followed by Anne, Elizabeth, Isabel, Mary, Barbara and Samuel. Tragically, Isabel and Barbara fell victim to a plague that ravaged Stathern in 1646, they died aged only eight and five.

Francis was chosen as Churchwarden in 1638 and 1639, although Gabriel Caunt acted for him. The Constables' Accounts for Stathern inform us that Francis was selected as the village constable on 5 April 1635. These accounts give a fascinating insight into village life during the early 17th century. His duties would have included collecting the Charles I ship money, a controversial and unpopular 'tax'. Another duty was to ensure ale brewed in the village was up to the assize standard and report to the justices of the peace.

Then there were the village soldiers... Arrangements needed to be made for training, usually at Loughborough or Leicester, and their armour needed to be kept in good condition. As a rule, the constable would escort the soldier and provide him with a horse and a hiring waggon to carry the baggage. The officers' fees needed to be paid and to those who acted as conductors as they travelled to the assembly place. In addition to this, gunpowder had to be made and badges provided to distinguish one set of soldiers from another.

The accounts record details of all monies paid out to poor and lame people, some of whom were passing through the village, and some interesting characters emerge through these records such as the moulde cachers (mole catchers). Repairs to the penfold and the church windows were frequent. The transcription of these accounts by Everard Guildford is well worth reading.

Francis was a wealthy landowner, essentially the squire of the village and a Justice of the Peace. He is described as a man of few words and also flawed, nevertheless, he was a deeply religious and loyal man.

Indeed, this devoutness at times caused conflict with his wife, Isabel, who in about 1655, turned to the Quaker faith and attended George Fox's meetings, the man who founded Quakerism. In fact, Francis was responsible for having Fox arrested a couple of times. But before this, one would like to imagine them living a peaceful countryside family life wealthy, prestigious and well-respected in the area. Then England was ripped apart by the outbreak of the Civil War in 1642.

The war can be divided into three stages: the first from 1642-1648, the second in 1649, and the third from 1650 -1651. Much is already written about Cromwell, Francis and the Civil War, and this narrative is only meant to briefly outline Francis's involvement in the conflict.

For reasons unknown, Francis took up the parliamentarian cause as opposed to his brothers, Thomas and Rowland, who fought for the king. Indeed, their father lent £1000 and was plundered of £4000 in support of the king. In 1643, Francis was commissioned as a captain commanding a troop of eighty men in a Regiment of Horse under Henry Grey of Burbage. He quickly proved himself to be a formidable fighter and soon became one of Oliver Cromwell's most trusted soldiers and confidantes.

The Constables' Accounts contain the names of various captains visiting Stathern and entries such as payment for a bed and vittles for a soldier who had brought a warrant. In 1643, two shillings were paid for Royalist soldiers *"that would have had horses when the Randevow was at our milne."*

Also, payments were made to Cromwell for supplies and ale while he was at Belvoir Castle, alongside a note suggesting that Cromwell would have stayed at Hacker's house in Stathern during this time, c. 1645.

On 27 November 1643, Francis was taken prisoner at Melton Mowbray but released a month later in exchange for a royalist colonel. Imprisoned again in 1645 after the Royalists had captured Leicester, he spent a lengthy stay in the dungeons of Belvoir Castle. During that time, he was offered his pardon and command of a regiment to change sides, only to refuse it with scorn, it is said. In 1648, Francis was made colonel and commanded the left wing of Colonel Rossiter's victorious parliamentary forces at Willoughby, Nottinghamshire.

Following the parliamentarian victory, Charles I was arrested and imprisoned. His trial took place in January 1649, *and on behalf of the people of England, the king was impeached 'as a Tyrant, Traitor, Murderer, and a public and implacable Enemy to the Commonwealth of England'.* He was sentenced to death, and a Death Warrant was drawn up and signed by fifty-nine commissioners or judges on 27 January 1649. Francis was <u>not</u> one of the signatories, but his name appears on the warrant as an addressee alongside Colonel Hunks and Colonel Phayre. Crucially, Francis did sign the execution warrant.

Francis was ordered to guard the king whilst he was imprisoned and escorted him to the platform where the executioner awaited to strike the fatal blow. His involvement in the king's execution proved to be his ultimate downfall. King Charles was beheaded on 30 January 1649. From then on, England, Wales and later Scotland and Ireland were governed as a republic and declared a Commonwealth.

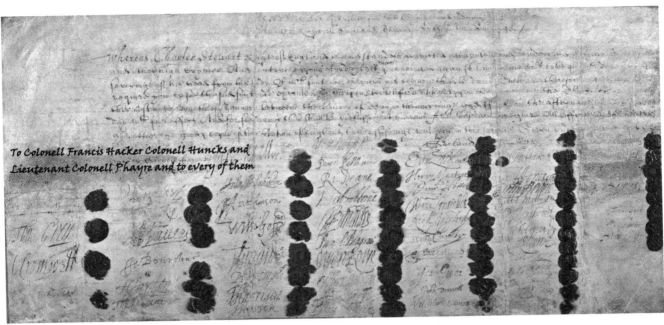

DEATH WARRANT FOR CHARLES I

The document was returned to the House of Lords on the 31 July 1660 and has been kept in the custody of Parliament ever since.

IMAGE DEPICTING THE BEHEADING OF CHARLES I FRANCIS HACKER IS PERSON **D** ON THE RIGHT

The Commonwealth period brought its own share of trials and tribulations to the English people, and trouble never really left Francis's doorstep. He continued to be called upon by Cromwell as part of the mechanism to keep law and order in the country. From 1650, Francis was heavily embroiled in the war with the Scots and commanded his Regiment of Horse at the Battle of Dunbar on 3 September 1650. The Scots were defeated and Francis was involved in the first stage of escorting 4,000 Scottish prisoners on a forced march from Dunbar to Berwick, where thirty of the prisoners were shot. Francis's escort was relieved at this point, and the march continued.

Consequently, he was barely at home with his family, and this is reflected in the Constables' Accounts where the last entry for him paying his levy was 1653. From 1655 to 1660, Edward Sheppardson had taken over as either the tenant or lessee of the farm at Stathern. Sheppardson was a captain in Francis's regiment and must have been a trusted friend. There is evidence showing them in business together at Harraton Colliery, near Sunderland in 1652.

Francis can be placed in Oakham, Rutlandshire in 1656 and 1658. In *The Parliamentary or Constitutional History of England Vol. 21,* his name is listed as one of the persons returned to serve in parliament. He is recorded as Col. Francis Hacker of Oakham and was paid £474 10s *(equivalent in 2022 = £91,1036)* per annum. This list also includes the names of the men who voted for Oliver Cromwell to be king. Francis was one of them.

In between his orders from Cromwell, and there is a possibility that he was also a spy, there are times when Francis was at home and continued his duties as a Justice of the Peace. In 1655, he is recorded solemnizing a marriage at Muston, Leicestershire and another in 1656 at Burrough-on-the-Hill.

Isabel's turn of faith to Quakerism is documented at this time, having become a follower of George Fox, one of the Quaker founders. In his diary, *The Journal of George Fox,* he writes that Isabel was at Whetstone, Leicestershire, in 1655 where she had attended a meeting and 'been convinced' (see page 25).

The Civil War is extremely complicated and Francis's involvement is well documented elsewhere, but when Oliver Cromwell died on 3 September 1658, parliament began to waver. His son Richard, succeeded in his place as Lord Protector, but he had no power base in parliament or the army. Still, he knighted Francis on 21 April 1659 *(Clarke's Papers Vol III p.191)* perhaps in an effort to gain Francis's

support. The Protectorate ended with Richard Cromwell's abdication on 25 May 1659. Chaos descended, and by December 1659, Francis's regiment was decommissioned and he was relieved of his command.

Francis returned home, and from document *E178/6285 at the National Archives* we learn that in May 1660, he began selling his livestock in Stathern. Perhaps he sensed trouble and wanted to be certain his family would be secure. He sold 350 sheep worth £175 *(equivalent in 2022 = £31,190) and nine heifers worth 40s (equivalent in 2022 = £356.40).* The money arising from the sales was paid to Isabel. A full transcription of the document can be seen in Appendix VI.

The collapse of the Commonwealth made way for the restoration of Charles II. He returned to England and entered London on 29 May 1660, his 30th birthday and was eventually crowned king at Westminster on 23 April 1661.

To seek justice for his father's death, Charles introduced the Indemnity and Oblivion Act of 1660. It was a general pardon to those who had committed crimes during the Civil War, except for crimes such as murder (without a licence granted by the King or Parliament), piracy, buggery, rape and witchcraft, and those involved in the regicide of Charles I. Of the 104 people excluded from the act, forty-nine named persons and the two unnamed executioners faced a capital charge. Of those listed to receive punishment, twenty-four had already died, including Oliver Cromwell, Henry Ireton and John Bradshaw, the

CHARLES II

32

judge who had been the court president. These men, together with Oliver Cromwell, were given posthumous executions. Their bodies were exhumed, hanged, beheaded and their remains cast into a pit below the gallows. Afterwards, their heads were stuck on spikes above Westminster Hall, the building where the High Court of Justice had sat for Charles I's trial. The heads remained there for all to see for many years.

On 5 July 1660, Francis was arrested and taken to the Tower of London where he awaited trial. At first, he was included in the general pardon, but during the court proceedings, it came to light that Francis had in his possession the Death Warrant signed by the fifty-nine commissioners and addressed to Francis. On 23 July 1660 there was an order for *the Lieutenant of the Tower to examine Colonel Hacker touching the original warrant for the King's execution, and to return the warrant to the House on the morrow.*

The day after, the Lieutenant of the Tower reported that Isabel and the family were in town and ordered - *That Colonel Hacker do forthwith send his Wife into the Country, to fetch the said Warrant; and that the Gentleman Usher attending this House do send a Man along with her for that Purpose.* (House of Lords Journal Vol. 11)

The warrant may have been kept at their home in the country for up to eleven years. On her return to London, Isabel delivered a strong testimony in the hope of saving her husband, but tragically, it was of no use. Francis's name was added to the list of those who had committed a non-exempt crime.

The following evidence is from a transcript of Francis's trial dated 15 October 1660:

We shall make it appear to you, that he was one of the persons that were upon the Guard, and kept the King a Prisoner, that he might be sure to be brought to that Mock Court of Injustice. Then it will appear to you, That this Prisoner at the Bar was highly trusted by all those Miscreants that thirsted for the Kings blood, by their bloody Warrant directed to him and others, to take the Kings person into custody, and to see Execution done. This was the person that kept him till he brought him to that fatal Stage. That this Warrant was lately brought from his own house by his own Wife to the House of Lords, and then we shall shew you that this person set his hand to the Warrant to the Executioner for Execution. That he did not do it ignorantly nor unwillingly, for he heard the Warrant read: we shall make it appear that he was upon the Scaffold, and had the Ax in his hand.

Then, to make matters worse later in the trial, Colonel Hercules Huncks revealed that he was with Cromwell, Hacker, Robert Phayer and Daniel Axtell on the day of the execution when Cromwell asked Huncks to write the warrant for the executioner. Huncks refused to do it. Cromwell *would have no delay* and hastily wrote the order himself and passed it to Francis to sign, which he did, thus sealing his fate.

"A internet search came across an interesting story about a man who purchased two 17th-century volumes on the regicide of Charles I. He made an astonishing discovery at the back of one of the volumes, it was a manuscript of the executioner's warrant. It was clearly a forgery (the year of the execution is wrong), but it seems possible that the forger may have had access to a similar document to base his forgery on."

He swore he did not know the executioner's name and had signed the paper without reading it. Francis had nothing with which to defend himself. He had signed the warrant to the executioner, although this was never produced in court, commanded the troops who marched Charles to Westminster to be executed and stood by the king's side as he was beheaded. To this day, the identity of the executioner remains unknown.

The only words Francis spoke in his defence were:

Truly my Lord, I have no more to say for myself, but that I was a Souldier and under command, and what I did was by that Commission you have read.

Francis was sentenced to death, and as a traitor, should have been hanged, drawn and quartered. Pleas by his brother, Rowland, for him only to be hanged were acknowledged, evidence of which can be found in the *Calendar of State Papers, Domestic, Charles II Vol. XVIII*, on 18 October 1660:

Axtell and Hacker are to suffer at Tyburn tomorrow, but the latter is only to be hanged, his body being begged.

And: *A Selection of Cases from the State Trials Vol Ii*

Where Hacker was only hanged, and his brother Rowland Hacker, had his body entire, which he begged.

The execution took place on 19 October 1660 at Tyburn Gallows. Francis was fifty-five years old, and it is uncertain where he was buried. Some say at the church of St. Nicholas Cole Abbey, London, the advowson of which was once vested in the Hacker family, although the advowson returned to the crown following Francis's death. No burial record can be found, therefore, no one can be sure, there is even some suggestion his body was taken back to Stathern, but again, it is only hearsay.

The heartbreak and devastation for Isabel and their children must have been almost impossible to bear and to break them further, Francis's estate was forfeited to the crown and given to the king's brother, James, the Duke of York.

Another legend passed down the waves of time comes into play now, that Stathern 'Hall' was demolished and that Isabel was allowed to live at Withcote Hall, Oakham, the home of Henry Smith. The problem here is that Smith was also a regicide, and his estate was likewise seized by the crown. It was granted to Edward Lord Hyde in March 1661 and then passed on to John Wilmot the Earl of Rochester. He tried to re-convey it to Sir Edward Smith, a member of another branch of the Smith

family, but he declined it on account of the disgrace of it being attached to a regicide. The Earl then sold it to Matthew Johnson, a clerk of the parliament.

Still, there is evidence putting Isabel at Withcote Hall on 27th February 1658. In *A Declaration to the Baptists Concerning the name of the Lord* by Humphry Wollwich printed in 1659, there is an account of a dispute with Baptists at Henry Smith's at Withcock, where Isabel Hacker signed as a witness.

Isabel and Francis are further evidenced in Oakham during the spring of 1660. Found in *The Christian Progress of that Ancient Servant and Minister of Jesus Christ* - the Memoirs of the Quaker minister George Whitehead...

There has been a Friends meeting in Peterborough where dirt and rotten eggs were thrown at him: he writes:

Next Morning, after I arose, Isabel Hacker, the wife of Col. Hacker (who had been at the said Meeting) bestowed some Labour to get out of my Hair, the Dirt which was thrown at me, the Day before, at the said Meeting. After that, I rode wither her and Company, **to Oucom [Oakham], to her House in Rutlandshire** *wither the Priest of the Town, (a great Presbyterian) came the next Day, with whom I had some Discourse, in the Presence of the said Col. Hacker, and the Priest being high and proud, was apt to get up in Passion, and Anger, which made him incapable of holding any fair Discourse; I told him of his Pasion, & c. which he would not acknowledge, but told me I was in Anger or Passion; because I spake somewhat zealously or earnestly to him, I told him he should not provoke me into Anger or Passion, if he should rail against me from Morning till Evening; so our Discourse quickly broke off, and I did not perceive that Col. Hacker, or any one present, could excuse the angry Priest.*

These references to the family in Oakham from about 1655, do conflict with the stories that Stathern 'Hall' was demolished following Francis's execution. Indeed, when the survey was carried out on Francis's house at Colston Bassett in September 1662, this note was added by the surveyor:

But as far as any lands or Tenements or Farmes in Statherne I can finde none, The Lease there held of the Earle of Rutland being Expired.

There is now a strong suggestion that the family had left Stathern and were living in Oakham, and the property in which they were living there was a leasehold, hence it was not seized. This now leaves us with not only the search for Stathern 'Hall' but also the search for Hacker's House in Oakham.

Following the Restoration, Charles II resumed the persecution of the Quakers, and Isabel's utter devotion to her faith ultimately led to her arrest on 14 December 1664. She was sentenced with a group of seven men and thirteen women to be transported to Jamaica for seven years, which was a virtual death sentence at that time. From *The Somerby Estate - Matt Philpott*, it is said that they lay packed on ship-board in the Thames before an order came for their release.

The brutal persecution of the Quakers is described in *The History and Antiquities of the County of Leicester, Vol, 2 part 1:* This entry comes under Claxton (Long Clawson): In 1674, John Marriott and William Parker were imprisoned, at the suit of Mr Reay, each of them for a year's tither. *Sufferings of Quakers, vol. I. p. 337* - Mr Reay was the vicar at Long Clawson for about sixty years.

And from *The Continued Cry of the Oppressed for Justice, 1675* by William Penn (1644-1718) the following disturbing account can be found:

For a meeting at Long Claxton, or Clawson, four persons were sent to prison, and so much goods at different times taken from some of the said meeting, that they had not a cow left to give the young children milk; their very bedclothes, and working tools, escaped not the violence, or avarice, of the persecutors; the total sum amounted to above £236 (equivalent in 2022=£37,740).

Nor did this satisfy our persecutors, for they cruelly dragged some women in the streets by the necks, till they were near stifled, tearing the clothes off their heads and backs. One woman that gave suck was so beaten and bruised on her breast, that it festered and broke, with which she had endured many weeks misery and torture; another woman of seventy-five years of age was violently thrown down upon the ground by one W. Guy, constable; the men were sorely beaten, drawn and dragged out of the meeting, some by the heels, some by the hair of the head, and some so bruised, that they were not able to follow their day-labour. Others they whipt in the face till the blood ran down; there was one they furiously trod upon, till the blood gushed out of his mouth and nose.

To complete the matter, the informers took away one of the prisoners his purse and money, as if he had not been a quiet neighbour, but a prisoner of war; nor was this accidental, but design, no short fit of cruelty upon an extraordinary provocation, for at this bitter rate they have treated them for several months. Witnesses, Edward Hallam, William Marriott, John Wilsford, William Smith, Richard Parker. Ibid.

"Isabel died in 1677 and her burial is recorded in the Quaker Records on 10 December 1677 at Stathern, although it is believed her body lies in the Quaker graveyard at nearby Long Clawson, Leicestershire. The location of which is believed to be in the orchard of The Homestead, Long Clawson, which was, or is on the site of an old Quaker Meeting House."

THE CHILDREN

The truth of how the children felt and coped after their father's death will never be known, but surviving records can give a glimpse of the lives some of them forged for themselves.

FRANCIS - ELDEST SON

Francis's story will be told in his own chapter.

SAMUEL - YOUNGEST SON

Information contained in Isabel Hacker's administration document held at the National Archives *Prob 6/53 f.85*, dated 1679, is where the discovery of Samuel, a previously unknown younger son of Isabel and Francis, was made. This was a remarkable find as nowhere in any of the reference material studied is his existence mentioned, however, further research has confirmed it is correct, and he has quite a story to tell.

Samuel was born about 1648. No baptism record for him can be found for him at St Guthlac's, Stathern, due to missing records. His name did not appear in 1647, and only one entry for 1648 is recorded.

The discovery of an apprenticeship record in the City of London Haberdashers Apprentices and Freemen database on *Findmypast* confirmed Samuel as Francis and Isabel's son.

Samuel Hacker son of Francis Hacker of Oakham in the county of Leicestershire yeoman put himself Apprentice to Michael [Stancliff] Haberdasher for seven years the date 3 June 1662

Samuel would be about fourteen years old, the perfect age for an apprenticeship, and it happens that Michael Stancliff was also a Quaker. It makes sense that Isabel would put her trust in her fellow Friends, and it transpires that the apprenticeship served Samuel very well indeed.

In 1681, Boyd's Inhabitants of London recorded Samuel living in St Lawrence Jewry, London as a citizen and haberdasher. He married twice, first to Elizabeth Byfield on 8 December 1681 at All Hallows, Staining, London. Samuel was aged about thirty-four, and Elizabeth aged nineteen. The couple had two daughters, Dorothy and Elizabeth, and a son, Francis, who would probably have been their first child. Sadly, he died very young and was buried on 27 August 1683 at St Lawrence, Jewry. His burial record reads that he was *interred in the little vault*. On 12 June 1695, Isabella Hacker was also interred in the little vault, who is most likely another daughter.

Daughter Dorothy married Giles Sadler on 15th June 1710 in London. Daughter Elizabeth was the second wife of Hugh Bateman, a solicitor from Derby, whom she married on 4 November 1724. She is incorrectly recorded as being <u>Mrs</u> Elizabeth Hacker in the All Saints, Breadsall, parish register. Hugh Bateman inherited the Hartington estate in Derby and later the Secheverall and Osborne estates in Derbyshire.

Samuel's second wife was Elizabeth Coupe, née Crompton, the relict of Henry Coupe or Coape, and he married her on 4 April 1711 at Allestree, Derby. Samuel was about sixty-four years of age, and Elizabeth thirty-three. They had a daughter, Hannah, born in 1713 at Duffield, Derbyshire.

In 1684, Samuel appeared in the London Gazette. Interestingly, as we shall learn later, his older brother, Francis, lived in Nottingham at this time.

Stolen out of Mr. Thomas Smiths shop at Nottingham, 42 pair of Womens Silk Hose, being 23 pair Green, 8 pair Mazarine Blue, 9 pair Pearl colour, 2 pair Philamot. If any of these Hose are offered to be pawned or sold, give notice to Mr. Samuel Hacker at the Bell in Lawrence Lane, London, they shall be rewarded for their pains: The weight is about 3 ounces with a Star Clock.

Philamot is known as Feuille Morte and is a brownish-orange colour.

ISABEL HACKER'S ADMINISTRATION ENTRY

Isabella Hacker On the 17th day was issued a commission to Samuel Hacker, natural and lawful son of Isabella Hacker late of Stathern in the County of Leicester, widow, deceased, having [goods and chattels in the Province of Canterbury] etc., having been sworn about well [and truly administering and making an inventory] etc., to administer the goods, rights and credits of the said deceased.

Translation from the Latin document kindly carried out by Peter Foden.

Samuel's name emerges on the Surrey and City of London Livery Company Association Oath Rolls. His oath year was 1696, and his title was 'livery.' Becoming a liveryman was the company's highest class and was granted to those who had set up business on their own, were freemen of the city, and had been admitted as full members of the company. They were also eligible to become members of the court eventually.

He passed away in 1723, aged about seventy-six, and was buried on 20 February at St Alkmunds, Duffield, Derbyshire. His burial entry records him as *Samuel Hacker, gent of Duffield*. He wrote a very long-winded will in 1722, a full transcription of which can be found in Appendix I. The wealth he had amassed enabled him to leave his wife £4000 *(£663,800 in 2022)* mainly as South Sea stocks. This wealth would be needed to pay a solicitor, who charged by the word in the Georgian period, to write out the will. His wife, Elizabeth's will was proved in 1757, and thankfully, it appears that she managed to maintain much of the wealth she inherited from Samuel.

At Linley Wood, Talke, Staffordshire, home of the Caldwell family, two large portraits of Samuel and Elizabeth hung there from the early 1800s until 1949. Samuel's wife, Elizabeth, was a great aunt to Elizabeth Caldwell. Samuel's portrait shows him in a full-bottomed wig of the Restoration Period. The portraits were possibly sold with the estate and their whereabouts are at present unknown.

At the age of about twelve, his father was executed as a traitor, so it is heart-warming to know that Samuel did incredibly well for himself after an event that might easily have ruined his chances in life.

"The direct line of Colonel Francis Hacker's male descendants ended with Samuel's death."

ANNE - ELDEST DAUGHTER

Anne was baptised at St Guthlac's, Stathern on 25 March 1634 and twenty-six when her father was executed. She was seemingly unmarried at the time, being one of the *utterly ruined* sisters (see page 43). At present, nothing more is known about her.

ELIZABETH - SECOND DAUGHTER

Elizabeth was baptised on 9 October 1637 at St Guthlac's, Stathern, and once more we must turn to the *Journal of George Fox* to learn more about her. In 1655, Fox had again been brought before Colonel Francis Hacker to be questioned regarding a plot against Oliver Cromwell and the Friends meetings that Fox is holding. During the questioning, a young man named Captain Clement Needham addresses Francis concerning Fox, and Fox writes:

Then his son Needham said, 'Father, this man hath reigned too long. It's time to have him cut off.' And I asked him for what; or what had I done or whom had I wronged from a child, for I was bred and born in that country, and who could accuse me of any evil from a child.

Needham was another trusted captain in Francis's Regiment of Horse and his son-in-law. There are suggestions that Needham married Anne, the eldest daughter, and perhaps some confusion has arisen with Hubbard's theory (see page 25). However, an

June 1662

Samuel Hacker son of ffrancis Hacker of Oakham in ye county of Leicester yeoman put himself Aprentice to Michell Stancliff Haberdasher for 7 years from ye date 3 June

REPRODUCTION OF SAMUEL'S APPRENTICESHIP RECORD

entry in the Stathern parish register on 26 November 1654, proves that Elizabeth was his bride.

Mary Needham the daughter of Clamman Needham, Gentleman and Elizabeth his wife, born betwixt two & three of clock in the after noune

No marriage record can be found, and she would have been seventeen years old when she gave birth to Mary. Tragically, their daughter only lived for a couple of months, she was buried on 23 January 1654 at Stathern. All was not lost though, they had another daughter Elizabeth. Her birth date is unknown, but she married on 21 August 1681 to Samuel Halford at St Peter's, Nottingham.

The next baptism found for the couple was for Clem Needham son of Clement on 27 February 1660 at Hoby, Leicestershire. He probably died young as he is not mentioned in his father's will. Further baptisms for their children were, Isabella, father Clement, mother Elizabeth, baptised on 9 May 1662, and Maria baptised on 2 December 1664, at St Michael and All Saints, Rearsby, Leicestershire

Further sadness befell the Hacker family when Elizabeth died aged only twenty-nine. She was buried on 2 December 1666 at Rearsby.

Clement married a second time in 1669 to a widow, Mary Clark, with whom he had a further four daughters, Mary, Anna, Martha and Deborah. Interestingly in his will, dated 1689, Clement leaves his daughters, Butler and Crisp, £5 (*£964.70 in 2022*) to *buy them mournings*. The poor girls are only known by their married surnames.

Well... Isabella married William Crisp in 1684, and records showed that Isabella died in 1698. Deborah married William Busby. Mary had died young in 1672, which left either Anna or Martha to have married Mr Butler. Unfortunately, no marriage record can be found for either of them.

Clement was another of Francis's trusted captains. Not only was he married to one of his daughters, he was recorded as the occupant at Colston Bassett in document *DD/4P/22/317-318* deposited at the Nottinghamshire Archives, dated November 1660 and May 1661. It is the enquiry and inquisition of various regicides including Francis. Further allies are placed in his other properties namely, William Skillington at Kneeton, William Ayliffe Gent. at East Bridgford and Penniston Whalley and Robert Alvey at Car Colston.

It appears that both Francis and Isabel drew their most trusted allies around them when they sensed the danger that came to pass after Cromwell's death. Francis chose his only companions, his soldiers, and Isabel her Quaker Friends.

ISABEL - THIRD DAUGHTER

Isabel was baptised on 24 January 1638 at St Guthlac's, Stathern, and her life was cut tragically short when 'plague' hit the village. She was buried on 30 April 1646, only eight years of age.

MARY - FOURTH DAUGHTER

Mary was baptised at Stathern on 8 March 1639, and twenty-one when her father was executed. She is the other *ruined* sister (see page 43). Sadly, no more is known about her either.

For now, the two sisters seem to have disappeared from history.

BARBARA - FIFTH DAUGHTER

Barbara was baptised on 18 July 1641 at Stathern and was also taken by 'plague'. She was buried the day before her sister, Isabel, on 29 April 1646. She was not quite five years of age.

In an abstract written by Stuart B Jennings, he writes:

With the surrender of the king in May 1646 the country looked forward to the ending of the Civil War and the social disruption it caused. It was hoped that commerce and trade would improve and travel restrictions be ended. Unfortunately, from 1645 onwards virulent pestilence and infection inflicted many of the formerly besieged towns and garrisons. The ending of the war allowed both discharged soldiers and civilians to wander across the country carrying the infections with them.

"This wave of infection could have been the one that reached Stathern and carried off seventeen people in the village, including Barbara and Isabel."

Rowland Hacker Full name of Husband	8 January 1610 St Mary the Virgin, Lowdham Baptism Date and Place
Francis Hacker His Father	Abt 1635-1640 Marriage Date and Place
Anne His Mother with Maiden Name	7 October 1674 St Peter's, East Bridgford Burial Date and Place
Unknown Full name of Wife	Unknown Birth Date and Place
Unknown Her Father	
Unknown Her Mother with Maiden Name	Before 1674 possibly before 1664 Death Date and Place

And The Children Were………………………

? Thomas   Born: before 1645   Buried: 11 Sep 1645
East Bridgford

1. Unknown   Born: before 1647   Buried: 1647
Stathern

2. Charles   Born: abt 1650   Married: Jane   Buried: 28 Apr 1719
East Bridgford

3. Ferdinando   Born: abt 1650s   Married: Katherin Trewel
17 Apr 1692
St Andrew's, Dublin, Ireland   Buried: Unknown

4. Mary   Born: abt 1650s   Married: Mr Westby   Buried: ?26 October 1711
Kinoulton

5. Sarah   Born: abt 1650s   Married: John Brough
3 May 1673
St Mary Magdalene's, Newark   Buried: 20 Dec 1695
East Bridgford

6. John   Born: Unknown   Buried: 29 Sep 1656
Houghton-on-the Hill, Leics
Son of Col. Hacker

7. Richard Dawson   Bapt: 29 Apr 1664   Colston Bassett - mother Anne Dawson

ROWLAND HACKER
1610 -1674

THE LAUGHING CAVALIER
BY FRANS HALS 1624

Rowland was baptised on 8 January 1610 at St Mary the Virgin, Lowdham, the youngest son of Francis Hacker and Anne. The monarch reigning at the time was James I of England, who also ruled as James VI of Scotland.

Although no record of a marriage for Rowland can be found, there must have been at least one Mrs Hacker, for he had six children that we know of, plus an illegitimate son. There is also a burial entry at East Bridgford on 11 September 1645, for Thomas Hacker, the son of Rowland and Elizabeth. This could suggest that his wife was named Elizabeth, however, it has to be considered that Thomas could have been the son of the older Rowland, who possibly married Elizabeth Yarborough. (see page 13). Unfortunately, a thorough search of parish records in the various villages in which the Hackers had property revealed nothing else to substantiate the theories, either there are gaps for the years required or no entries for Hackers at all. So, this too remains a mystery...

Four children are mentioned in Rowland's will, dated 1673, Charles, Ferdinando, Mary and Sarah, and they were probably born during the 1640s to 1650s. One of his other children's existence came to light in the Stathern Churchwardens Accounts Vol. 2, when in 1647: *6s 8d paid by Rowland Hacker for the burial of his child in the church.*

Frustratingly, the child's name is unknown as the Stathern burial records for 1647 are incomplete.

A burial at St Mary's, Houghton-on-the Hill, Leicestershire, informs the possibility of a further son. *John Hacker buried 29 September 1656, the son of Colonel Hacker.* The problem here is that both Rowland and his brother, Francis, attained the rank of colonel, so it is difficult to decide which of them was John's father. Francis can be placed in Oakham in 1656 and would also have been fighting the Scots during this period of time, whereas Rowland's involvement in any fighting had already ceased, making it more probable that he was John's father.

But what is the connection with Houghton-on-the-Hill? More on that later.

Alongside the children already mentioned, the Archdeaconry Records revealed yet another son. Rowland was presented on 29 April 1664 for *fornication with Anne Dawson, a widow at Colston Bassett and having a bastard child.* Scandalous!

There is a baptism at St John the Divine, Colston Bassett for Richard Dawson on 27 March 1664 - mother Anne Dawson, but no father is recorded. Rowland would have been about fifty-four years old, and whether he acknowledged the child is unknown, as he was not bequeathed anything in his will.

The sparse information pertaining to Rowland and his children is incredibly frustrating. The absence of parish records during the Commonwealth Period (1649-1660) is widespread across all counties and makes genealogy somewhat of a challenge during

John Hacker Son of Colonel Hacker September 29 : xxix

this time. Many records were destroyed in the Civil War period, and marriages could no longer take place in church. The 1653 Marriage Act stated a marriage had to take place before a Justice of the Peace. Nevertheless, 'banns' had to be read to announce an intention to marry on three consecutive Sundays after morning service or in the marketplace. The recording of marriages, births and deaths, not baptisms and burials, was the role of the 'Register', elected by the local ratepayers and approved by the JP. The 'Register' could be the local clergyman, as he might be the only person available who could read and write, and since small parishes could share a 'Register', the result was that some parishes recorded no marriages at all for this period while others increased dramatically simply because it was their clergyman who was responsible for keeping the book for the whole district. Many couples did not like the new system and secretly married in church if the clergy had managed to stay in office.

The 1653 Act declared that after 29 September 1653, no other form of marriage would be valid, but this clause was omitted four years later. At the Restoration of Canon Law in 1660, the validity of marriages celebrated before JPs needed to be confirmed. The importance of this little diversion in the rules governing marriages is that following the restoration, marriages before JPs were just legalised in retrospect. Some clergy refused to accept such blasphemy and forced a second marriage in the church or simply branded their children illegitimate. This bit of history helps explain the entries and remarks in some parish registers, such as *'Franklin alias Cox'* or *'Smith alias Jones'*. Very few Register's

records survived, therefore, many marriages during this period cannot be found unless they were one of those who remarried in church.

Whereas baptismal, marriage and burial records are difficult to find, the Hackers' involvement in the English Civil War is etched in history. The war brought grief and heartbreak to all families, both rich and poor. Rowland, like his brother, Thomas, also supported the king's army and spent much of the war attached to the Royalist Newark Garrison, first with Sir Richard Byron's Regiment of Horse and secondly with General Harry Hastings. In 1644, Rowland was made governor of the fort at Trent Bridge, West Bridgford, Nottingham, and was involved in a third attempt by the Royalists to capture Nottingham in February 1644. A planned surprise incursion was foiled by Cornet Palmer, who had been held prisoner at Newark. Having escaped, he fled to Nottingham to tell the castle garrison of the Royalists' plan. The event was captured in Lucy Hutchinson's diary, where she wrote that Rowland had *'chosen thirty of their men who, in disguises, should come like women and market people, and with long knives, daggers, hatchets and such kind of weapons as had under their cloaks.'*

Lucy was the wife of Colonel John Hutchinson, the parliamentarian commander of Nottingham Castle. The Parliamentarians, however, were waiting and chased the raiders back across Trent Bridge. Ten of their number were forced into the river below, five of the men drowned, four were captured, and one managed to swim to freedom.

In 1644, Rowland was gravely wounded in a minor skirmish near Leicester whilst serving with General Hastings, and it was thought he might die.

Thankfully, he survived but lost his hand, and some accounts say his arm.

NEWARK CASTLE

Despite his injury, he was promoted to colonel in 1645 and given command of a defensive outpost at Wiverton Hall, Nottinghamshire, which he eventually surrendered to General Sydenham Poyntz in November 1645. The hall was immediately demolished. From there, Rowland probably returned to the Royalist garrison at Newark, where on 26 November 1645, troops from Scotland started to besiege Newark from the north while Parliamentarian forces did the same from the south. The war was not going well for the

Royalists, and on 6 May 1646, the king ordered Newark garrison to surrender. Two days later, the troops marched out.

Following the surrender, and the end of the Civil War in 1649, Rowland would have sworn his oath not to take up arms against Parliament again, and he seemed to fall back into a peaceful life. But where? The burial records for three of his children in different villages suggest he did not appear to have a permanent home.

Part of the problem lay with his father only bequeathing Rowland *Twenty Pounds per annum (£3024 in 2022) of lawfull English money out of my Lands tenements and hereditaments in Kinholton to bee paid unto him by even and equall portions att the two most usuall feasts of St Michaell the archangel and the Annuntiation of the Blessed Virgin Mary the first payment to begin the first of the feasts Daies which shall first happen next after my Decease.*

Essentially, Rowland had no property of his own, and this had serious repercussions after his brother, Francis, was executed. With all of Francis's property seized, the rest of the family was left in a very dire situation.

The will was proved in 1647 as it had been written in 1640, by which time Thomas had been killed. In November 1660, a month after Francis was executed, Rowland was granted administration of the unadministered goods of his father. The term 'administration' is used in this context where there is no valid executor, but the rest of the will is valid. The surviving administration is held at the National Archives and indicates that Francis and Thomas, who were named as executors, had not completed their responsibilities in that role, and were both now deceased. In fact, Thomas had not even been sworn in. It appears as if Rowland was attempting to claw back the unadministered part of his father's goods. What these were is unknown at the time of writing.

In the Calendar of State Papers during the reign of Charles II, petitions by Rowland can be found that read:

October 1660 - Col. Rowland Hacker. For a grant of the estate of his brother, Col. Francis Hacker, convicted for treason, whereby the estate is forfeit and the family and two sisters utterly ruined. His father, Francis, being a loyal subject to the late King, lent him £1,000 (£159,700 in 2022) and was plundered of £4000 (£638,900 in 2022). His younger brother was slain in the service, and the petitioner was an active commander and lost the use of a hand - Certificate by Lord Langdale and five others, in favour of the petitioner.

The *two sisters utterly ruined* must have been Anne and Mary, the girls who cannot be accounted for. (see pages 37-38)

And:

January 1661 - Petition of Col. Rowland Hacker to the King for restoration of the whole or part of the estate of his eldest brother Fras. Hacker, lately executed for rebellion. His father, Fras Hacker, left portions therefrom for his younger children; he also lent the late King £1000 and spent money in horses and arms to promote the Royal interest.

Certificate by Gervase Holles and three others in favour of the petitioner, who was governor of Weverton House, kept Nottingham Bridge and showed much discretion and courage in the cause of the late King

Thoroton wrote that the Duke of York *favourably sold* some of the confiscated properties to Rowland, including the property at Colston Bassett, which was later purchased by John Grubham Howe of Langar. In 1662, the Colston Bassett estate totalled 383 acres and was valued at £213 9s 4d *(£31,720 in 2022)* although this figure does not take into consideration inflated property prices.

The question here is, where did Rowland acquire the money to purchase the properties? At present, this remains unanswered. However, another question to raise is, how did Rowland persuade Charles II not to have Francis hanged, drawn and quartered? Of the regicides put to death, he was the only one just hanged. If Charles were to make an example of any man, surely he would choose one who signed the execution order and was present on the platform at his father's beheading, but he did not. And even though Rowland reached the rank of colonel, he was still a relatively ordinary soldier in the Royalist Army, suggesting he was in considerable favour with the king in some other way. In contrast, Francis was deemed to be one of the foremost colonels in the Parliamentary Army. The possibility of involvement with the Sealed Knot now comes into play.

The Sealed Knot was a secret Royalist association which plotted for the Restoration of the Monarchy during the English Interregnum. The group was commissioned by King Charles II between November 1653 and February 1654 from his exile in Paris, to coordinate underground Royalist activity in England and prepare for a general uprising against the Protectorate. Its founder members were: John Belayse, Sir Willian Compton, Henry Hastings, Col. John Russell, Sir Richard Willis and Col. Sir Edward Villiers.

The Sealed Knot made ten attempts between 1652 and 1659 to bring about the Restoration, and the largest uprisings were staged in 1655 and 1659: The Penruddock uprising (1655) was named after one of the revolt's leaders, John Penruddock.

The revolt was easily put down by forces loyal to the Lord Protector Oliver Cromwell, and for his part in the rebellion, Penruddock was beheaded in May 1655. The conspiracy was ultimately ineffective, partly because of an abundance of caution, but not least due to the treachery of Willis, who was feeding information to Cromwell's spymaster John Thurloe from at least 1656, for reasons which remain unknown.

Booth's uprising (1659) occurred after the death of Oliver Cromwell. The conspiracy was known to Thurloe, and the Royalists under the command of Sir George Booth were militarily defeated on 19 August at the Battle of Winnington Bridge by a New Model Army contingent under the command of General John Lambert.

Source: Wikipedia

Interestingly, Richard Willis was Governor of Newark Castle during 1645, where he and Rowland would have crossed paths.

Intriguingly, Edward Villiers lived at Baggrave Hall, Leicestershire, only a few miles from Houghton-on-the-Hill, where the child, John Hacker, was buried in 1656, who may have been Rowland's son.

Was Rowland involved in the Sealed Knot and engaged in covert business with Villiers at Baggrave Hall? Although there is no evidence to support the theory, he was loyal to the king, he did beg for his brother not to be drawn and quartered, and succeeded, and was permitted to buy back some of the confiscated property. Food for thought, maybe.

Following this repurchase of properties, Rowland lived at Colston Bassett. The 1664 Hearth Tax return for the village is badly damaged, however, there is a Mr Hack… charged 22s, and it is the second largest house. Furthermore, he fathered his bastard child there in the same year which strongly suggests the Mr Hack… is Rowland.

No Hackers were recorded in East Bridgford in 1664 but in 1674, Rowland was taxed there for seven hearths. In 1677. When Volume I of Thoroton's History of Nottinghamshire was published, he wrote that Rowland was the present owner of the East Bridgford estate, *who by the favor of his Royal Highness the Duke of York, who sold him his Brother the said Francis his Estate,* although Thoroton must have visited East Bridgford prior to Rowland's death in 1674.

However, in Volume II of Thoroton's History of Nottinghamshire, issued in 1790, notes were added by John Throsby. He writes:

Colonel Rowland Hacker, after the death of his brother, left the King's Army in disgust, and died in retirement, upon a large leasehold property at East Bridgeford, which he had of the Masters, Fellows &c, of Magdalen College, Oxford.

Confirmation that Rowland did indeed own a leasehold from Magdalen College was found in a small document, featured right, dated 1668, listing chief rents in the manor of East Bridgford. Rowland is the chief tenant and is receiving rent from his son Charles and other men in the village. Whether this included the large house is uncertain.

Arthur Du Boulay Hill, author of *East Bridgford, a Notts. Village, 1932,* believed that Rowland's property was Burneham House, now the Old Manor House, on Main Street/College Street corner, which was originally built in about 1530.

REPRODUCTION OF THE 1664 HEARTH TAX
Showing the hole by the side of Mr Hacker's name

44

DOCUMENT 109/42 MAGDALEN COLLEGE
Reproduced with the kind permission of Dr Richard Allen

The manor of East Bridgford was held by Ralph, Lord Cromwell. It was acquired by Dr William Waynflete, Bishop of Winchester, for Magdalen College but the title to the property was disputed c. 1486 by Francis, Lord Lovell. In return for the surrender of the manor of Doddington, Northants, the College was able to secure Lovell's confirmation of its title to East Bridgford.

Returning to the Old Hall. It is known that from about 1649, three years after Francis Hacker I died, the hall was occupied by Dr Gilbert Sheldon and Mrs Okeover. Again, Thoroton is the source of this information.

To this House in Bridgeford did Dr. Gilbert Sheldon, then Warden of All-Souls College in Oxford, now Lord Archbishop of Canterbury, retire with old Mrs. Okeover, shortly after the Parliament's Commissioners had put him out of his Place in that University, and continued here three or four Years, well pleased with the River and Fields, and honored by the Neighbourhood, to all which he was ever very extraordinarily kind, and from myself, amongst the rest, deserves a better Acknowledgement.

By 1660, document *DD/4P/22/317-318* (see page 38) tells us that William Ayliffe is the occupant, and although the document is in Latin, the words a 'capital' messuage can be made out. Meaning a house together with its yard, outbuildings and lands.

Rowland was buried on 7 October 1674 at East Bridgford, and in his will, he expresses his desire to be buried in the north quire. No wife is mentioned, so it can be assumed she died before Rowland, although she seems somewhat of an enigma. He bequeaths his lands and properties in East Bridgford and Kinoulton to his son Charles, except for one cottage and a close called Spencers Wong that is given to his son, Ferdinando, who also receives £300 (£47,970 in 2022).

To his daughters, Mary Westby and Sarah Brough, he gifts money. Despite knowing the girls' married names, only a marriage record for Sarah has been found. She married John Brough of Derby by licence on 3 May 1673 at St Mary Magdalene, Newark.

Amongst their children, they had the delightfully named son, Hacker Brough, who became rector at Trowell. Sarah was buried at East Bridgford on 20 December 1695, as the wife of John.

Sadly, very little is known about Mary, another victim of missing records. However, there is a burial at St Luke's, Kinoulton where the Hackers had lands, for a Mary Westby, widow, on 26 October 1711, which might be a possibility.

Rowland's eldest son, Charles, married Jane in about 1675, and they had three children. Charles Jnr was born in 1676, followed by Orlando in 1679 and then Elizabeth in 1682, all at East Bridgford. The old hall there had been built in the 16th century, and Charles had it rebuilt in about 1690. It remained in the Hacker family for the next 200 years.

Charles died in 1719 and was buried at East Bridgford on 28 April. Jane passed away a few months later and was also buried at East Bridgford on 14 February 1720 .

As for Ferdinando, he travelled far and wide. In 1671/2 his name appeared on a passenger list to Virginia and then on a return trip to London aboard the *Fairfax* in 1679.

It looks very much like he was also involved in the tobacco trade, and his name appears in the *Kings' Remembrances Port Books*, a type of customs record, on 31 July 1685:

Shipper by the *Hopewell* of Boston, Mr Samuel Vesey, bound from Hull for New England: Ferdinando Hacker.

(document reference - *PRO: E190/328/1*)

Perhaps Ferdinando worked with his cousin, Francis, the extremely wealthy merchant in London mentioned earlier (see page 14). Indeed, in 1619 in order to maintain tight control over excise, King James I ordered that London was the only port into which tobacco could enter the country, and much wealth could be made at this time.

There is a marriage for a Ferdinando Hacker and Katherin Trewel on 17 April 1692 at St Andrew's, Dublin, Ireland. There is no other evidence to support the union, and sadly, the records go cold after this.

"Rowland conjures up the image of a typical dashing Cavalier. Fiercely loyal to the monarchy, yet tolerant of his parliamentarian brother. At his death, Rowland had restored the Hacker family name to gentry level. In reality, the Hackers were one of many families deeply divided by loyalties to opposing sides of a bloody war that took more lives proportionally than those lost in World War I."

Brief History of the Tobacco Trade

Sir Francis Drake first introduced tobacco to England in 1573, but British sailors had obtained tobacco for chewing or smoking from Spanish and Portuguese sailors even before then.

Drake discovered a method of curing the tobacco so it could be stored, transported and affordable. The formation of The East India Company made tobacco more widely available. Soon, the exchequer was enjoying considerable revenues from taxing the huge increase in the popularity of smoking.

17TH-CENTURY SHIP

Tobacco grew well in southern America, and typically Virginia, but farmers required capital to grow it, and during the 17th century, farmers saw it more as a temporary crop to start them off before they could plant something else. They reasoned that tobacco sold for pennies per pound, which was unprofitable. The solution to this problem was slavery.

Due to the low birth rate of European settlers in America, slavery helped keep costs down, increase profits and enable a change from small farms to larger ones. Those who created the large plantations in the fertile regions were highly prosperous even with the low price per pound of tobacco. Most slaves were treated reasonably well as it cost the farmers more to replace a slave than to keep the ones they already owned alive.

In the late 17th century, Caribbean farmers had the same idea of creating large farms using slaves. Here too, they were treated better than those working on the sugar plantations, as many came from African regions that grew tobacco and had experience planting and harvesting it.

"The Hacker family may well have continued in the tobacco trade, and evidence of this will be revealed later."

The **Hacker** Family

Francis Hacker III Physician/Extra LRCP Full name of Husband	26 May 1633 St Guthlac's, Stathern, Leics Baptism Date and Place
Francis Hacker His Father	9 Feb 1672 St Botolph's, London Marriage Date and Place
Isabel Brunts His Mother with Maiden Name	13 Mar 1693 St Antholin's, London Burial Date and Place
Anne Wolfris Full name of Wife	9 Mar 1654 St Olave's, Hart St. London Baptism Date and Place
John Wolfris His Father	
Alice His Mother with Maiden Name	Post 1715 Burial Date and Place

And The Children Were............................

1. **Anne**   Bapt: 23 Mar 1673
Stathern
   Married: Luke Denton
   9 Sep 1701
   St Mary le Strand, London
   Died: Unknown

2. **Francis IV**   Bapt: 22 Jun 1676
Stathern
   Married: never married
   Buried: 22 Oct 1715
   St Dunstan in the West, London

3. **John Wolfris**   Bapt: 10 Jul 1682
St Mary's, Nottingham
   Married: Susannah Cooks
   April 1712
   All Hallows, London
   Died: 1733-34,
   Jamaica

4. **Elizabeth**   Bapt: 18 Jun 1684
St Mary's, Nottingham
   Married: Anthony Lynch
   20 Jan 1703
   St Ann's, Blackfriars, London
   Died: after 1726

FRANCIS HACKER III
1633 -1693

Francis was baptised on 26 May 1633 at St Guthlac's, Stathern, the firstborn child of Francis Hacker and Isabel Brunts. The monarch reigning at the time was Charles I.

On 28 March 1649, at the age of sixteen, he entered Peterhouse College, Cambridge University. His Alumni entry records him as being educated at school in Coventry, adding that he was the son of Francis, Parliamentary Colonel and regicide and held a commission in his father's regiment. It would appear that this was young Francis's legacy. Interestingly, he did not matriculate. He entered university just three months after Charles I was executed, and it almost makes you feel as if everything was 'normal' following such a monumental event as England entered the Commonwealth Period.

Then, a surprising entry in Munk's Roll at the Royal College of Physicians (RCP) revealed that Francis Hacker of Nottingham was licenced Extra LRCP on 8 January 1686. Francis was a doctor, a physician.

Francis did not stay long at Cambridge, and until the middle of the 19th century, medicine was studied by only one or two students a year. This being the case, it is possible he studied medicine at one of the European universities, accounting for the ten-year gap before he joined his father in the army.

On 8 June 1659, aged twenty-six, he was commissioned to the rank of cornet in his father's Regiment of Horse. At this point in the Commonwealth period, Oliver Cromwell had died, and his son, Richard, had already 'abdicated' with Parliament resuming power as a prelude to the restoration of Charles II.

Within a few weeks, Francis was made lieutenant and then captain-lieutenant in Colonel Thomas Saunders' regiment. It was a time of enormous unsettlement, as it appeared that factions of the New Model Army forces loyal to different generals, might wage war on each other. Added to this, the public was now beginning to resent the strict Puritanism of the military leaders. A year later, Charles II was restored as king, the New Model Army was disbanded, and Francis's father was dead; hanged as a traitor.

The tragic events of 1660 undoubtedly affected the Hacker family deeply. Francis was twenty-seven years old and unmarried at this point in time. Where was he to live, and what would he do with his life?

Part of the answer to these questions lies within the Churchwardens' Accounts. These show that from 1661 to 1677 Francis paid a levy for land, beasts and sheep in Stathern. Indeed, within a year, Francis's levy doubled from 4s 8d on 28 October 1661 to 8s 4d on 6 January 1662, which was the greatest amount out of the inhabitants, all of whom paid this levy to the churchwardens. Also, in May 1662 he is charged for three hearths, the second largest house in the village, and recurs in the 1664 Hearth Tax.

At the age of thirty-nine, Francis married eighteen-year-old Anne Wolfris, on 9 February 1672 at St Botolph's, London. Their first two children were baptised in Stathern, Anne on 23 March 1673, followed by Francis on 22 June 1676. The younger children were baptised at St Mary's, Nottingham, namely John Wolfris on 10 July 1682 and Elizabeth on 18 June 1684.

Francis may well have worked as a local physician while he lived at Stathern, it would certainly account for some of his wealth. When Francis applied for his extra LCRP licence, he was fifty-two years old, which

THE PHYSICIAN'S VISIT
Jan Steen

seemed rather late in life, however, an enquiry to Felix Lancashire - Assistant Archivist at the RCP, resolved this.

The date given is the date that Dr Hacker passed his ExLRCP exam and was admitted to the RCP as an extra licentiate. (Extra licentiate was the term used for physicians practicing outside of London; within London, they were simply called licentiates.) The date was 8 January 1686 by modern dating.

He may well have been practising for many years prior to this. Even though at the time all physicians in England were technically obliged to apply for a licence to practise from either the RCP or the Church of England, most physicians did not bother with either. The RCP only tended to prosecute physicians for practising without a licence if they were based in London and had been accused of causing harm to their patients. It may be that Dr Hacker decided to apply for an ExLRCP qualification to improve his professional standing in Nottingham, or for his own personal satisfaction.

Francis applied for his licence a year after the birth of his youngest child in 1684, and perhaps now he was a respectable married man with a family he did wish to improve his professional standing. It also coincided with the family's move to London, where it was required for a physician to have a licence. It was also the same year when his younger brother, Samuel, was appealing for the whereabouts of the stolen stockings in Nottingham. (See page 36)

Francis wrote his will in 1685, eight years before his death. He named himself as *I Francis Hacker of the town and county of the town of Nottingham, gent.*, and continues to say that he is of sound mind and in a good state of health, *yet considering that I am naturally borne to dye and the great uncertainty of human life and how frequently men are surprised by an unexpected and sudden death,* he wishes to dispose of his estate.

He gives his beloved wife, Anne, property and lands in Stathern, alongside the windmill that stood at the top of Mill Hill, and a house called the Hall House, which is a style of house, containing about four acres. This is most probably the freehold property that had belonged to his father. On Anne's decease, the estate was to pass to their eldest son, Francis IV. A full transcript of the will can be found in Appendix I.

Francis died in 1693 and was buried at St Antholin's, London, on 13 March 1693. His children's marriages all took place in London.

It has proved difficult to locate a burial for his wife, Anne, as there are numerous possibilities amongst the London burials. The various spellings of Hacker, Hawker, Hooker etc, make it extremely challenging with no other records to cross reference. She was certainly still living in 1715, as she is mentioned in the will of her son, Francis IV, dated that same year.

Anne was also left an annuity of £4 (£636.70 in 2022) per annum by Samuel Brunts in 1712, who named her *Anne Hacker of London, my cousin the widow of Francis Hacker.* Samuel Brunts was the founder of the school in Mansfield, now known as the Brunt's Academy.

The lack of parish records pertaining to Samuel's birth makes it unclear how the cousin relationship links up, but he would be from the same generation as Isabel Brunts.

THE CHILDREN

ANNE - ELDEST DAUGHTER

Anne was baptised on 23 March 1673 at Stathern and married Luke Denton on 9 September 1701 at St Mary le Strand, London. No baptisms appear in the registers for any children born to the couple, but a short sentence in a will found in the database of American wills proved in London provided a possible reason. In 1733, a John Denton left an exceedingly long will, in which a beneficiary receives *the portion left to me by my brother Luke Denton before he went to the East Indies.*

The East Indies islands were coveted for their rich natural resources, including rubber, spices, cotton, and indigo. Their strategic locations were vital as important trading centres along the spice routes as Europe colonised the East Indies. The founding of various European trading companies during the 17th century, and the power of these trading companies, such as the East India Company, influenced the colonies' names, namely the British East Indies (India and Malaysia), the Dutch East Indies (Indonesia) and the Spanish East Indies (Philippines).

The East India Company yielded immense power in England, and its politics were complicated. However, the successful merchants who traded were rich, and whether Luke Denton was a merchant or a local governor in India or elsewhere is unknown. What happened to Luke and Anne in the East Indies will no doubt remain undiscovered as well.

EAST INDIA COMPANY COAT OF ARMS

FRANCIS IV - ELDEST SON

Sadly, this Francis's life was cut relatively short. He was baptised on 22 June 1676 at Stathern, and no marriage record for him can be found.

There is, however, a will written two weeks before he died, suggesting he might have fallen ill, as he was only thirty-nine years old.

He was buried on 22 October 1715 at St Dunstan-in-the-West, London. No wife is mentioned, and he makes his mother, Anne, his executrix, to whom he bequeaths his personal estate alongside the lands and properties at Stathern. He adds that two years after his death, she can raise money out of the rents on the properties to the sum of £50 (£7.949 in 2022) for her own use.

He pays his debts and gives his sisters Anne Denton and Elizabeth Lynch a *guinea a piece to buy them a Ring*. (Guinea = £166.90 in 2022)

Presumably, Anne and Luke had not left for the East Indies at this point in time.

Returning to the property at Stathern, further research revealed that the windmill had changed hands before 1730.

In the will of William Barnes of Stathern dated 1737, he gives his brother £30 (£5,109 in 2022) that had been lent to *the late Matthew Bull on a mortgage upon the Wind Mill at Stathern.*

Matthew Bull had died in 1730.

JOHN WOLFRIS - SECOND SON

John was baptised on 10 July 1682 at St Mary's, Nottingham, and he married Susannah Cooks at All Hallows, London, on 5 April 1712. No records for any children can be found in England, and there might be an answer to that.

A connection with far-flung shores seems to be a theme with this generation of our Hacker family. Found in the *Country Apprentices, West Indies database (Findmypast)* John Wolfris is listed as employing an apprentice named Edward Diss in 1711. John's occupation as the master is Merchant, his place, Jamaica, West Indies.

A dissertation written in 2006 titled *Christian Liturgy and the creation of British slave societies 1650-1780 By Nicholas M. Beasley*, contains the following passage: *Kingston paid an attorney for drawg the Articles of Agreement between John Hacker & the Vestry to make a Negro Markett place in 1730. Whites complained that Afro-Barbadians used Sunday for drumming, dancing, and riot, practicing frenzied incantations over the graves of their deceased.*

It is alarming today to think that John might have been involved in the slave trade, but the sad fact is, in this period of history, money was to be made in the abysmal business.

In the *Index of Early Wills of Jamaica*, John is recorded as leaving a will in 1733-34.

ELIZABETH - SECOND DAUGHTER

Elizabeth was baptised on 18 June 1684 at St Mary's Nottingham, and she married Anthony Lynch of Codicote, Hertfordshire, a clerk, on 20 January 1703, at St Ann's Blackfriars, London.

Anthony Lynch of Codicott in Hartfordshire, Clerk, and Elizabeth Hackers of St Holbourn, London

Anthony was Rector of St Peter & St Paul's in Shalden, Hampshire, until his death in 1725. A bond for the administration of his estate was granted to Elizabeth on 3 February 1726, but there is no burial record for Elizabeth to be confident of.

"And so, this account of the direct ancestors and descendants of Francis Hacker, parliamentarian and regicide, concludes."

✚ 1549 - Book of Common Prayer was first issued, and it was officially known as the First Prayer Book of Edward VI

✚ 1553 - Lady Jane Grey is proclaimed Queen. After nine days, Mary (half-sister of Elizabeth I) arrives in London, Lady Jane Grey is arrested and Mary is crowned. She is also known as 'Bloody Mary'

✚ 1554 - the persecution of Protestants begins, heresy laws are revived and England is returned to Catholicism

✚ 1556 - Thomas Cranmer, Archbishop of Canterbury is burned at the stake for heresy

✚ 1558 - Elizabeth accedes to the throne after the death of Mary I, and the following year is made head of the Church of England

✚ 1563-4 - 17,000 die of the Plague in London

✚ 1568 - Mary Queen of Scots flees to England and is imprisoned by Elizabeth

✚ 1577-80 Francis Drake sails around the world

✚ 1578 - Humphrey Gilbert and Walter Raleigh set out from Plymouth leading an expedition to establish a colony in North America; forced to turn back six months later

✚ 1580 - Construction of Wollaton Hall, Nottingham started

✚ 1582 - Edinburgh University is founded

✚ 1586 - Thomas Harriot returns from a voyage to Colombia with the first potatoes seen in England

✚ 1587 - Mary Queen of Scots is executed

✚ 1588 - The Spanish Armada is defeated

✚ 1590 - North Berwick witch trials - James VI sets up royal commissions to hunt down witches in his realm, recommending torture in dealing with suspects

✚ 1595-6 - Walter Raleigh makes his first expedition to South America

✚ 1595 - Sir Francis Drake and Sir John Hawkins depart from England on their final voyage to the Spanish Main, which ends in both of their deaths

✚ 1602 - The United East India Company is formed

✚ 1603 - Elizabeth I dies at Richmond Palace, Surrey without an heir to the throne

✚ 24 March 1603 - James VI of Scotland takes the English throne

✚ 1605 - The Gunpowder Plot attempts to blow up the Houses of Parliament

✚ 25 September 1615 - Arbella Stuart, 'The Lost Queen' dies in the Tower of London. Bess of Hardwick was her grandmother

✚ 23 April 1616 - Death of William Shakespeare

✚ 1618 - Sir Walter Raleigh is executed for alleged treason at Westminster

✚ 1620 - The Pilgrim Fathers set sail for America aboard the *Mayflower*

✚ 1625 - Charles I accedes to the throne on the death of his father James I

✚ 1628 - The Petition of Right - a declaration of the 'rights and liberties of the subject' is presented to the King, who agrees to it under protest

✚ 1629 - Charles dissolves Parliament and rules by himself until 1640

✚ 1635 - The Royal Mail service is made available to the public by Charles I

✚ 1637 - The Scots sign the National Covenant when Charles tries to force a new prayer book on them

✚ 1640 - Charles summons Short Parliament, which lasts three weeks and Long Parliament which lasts until 1660

✚ 1641 - The Star Chamber and Court of High Commission are both abolished

✚ 1642 - Charles attempts to arrest five MPs and fails

✚ 1642-9 Civil War

✚ 30 January 1649 - Charles I was beheaded

✚ 1660 - Restoration of Charles II

✚ 19 October 1660 - Francis Hacker executed

✚ 1666 - The Great Fire of London

✚ 1733/34 - John Wolfris Hacker dies in Jamaica, the last known male in Francis Hacker I's line

APPENDIX I

LAST WILLS AND TESTAMENTS

MARGARET HACKER

23 June 1625

Proved 6 March 1628 Nottinghamshire

In the name of God Amen the 23rd daye of June in the firste year of the raign of our Sovraigne Lorde Charles by the grace of God Kinge of England Scotland and Ireland ... 1625: I Margaret Hacker of East Bridgford in the Countye of Nottingham beinge of good & pfect memorie thanks be too God therefore I doe ...God ... ... mee so to doo ... pnounce & declare this my laste will and testament in manner and forme following: First I commend my soule into hands of Almightie God ... to be made *partaker* of the Kingdome of Heaven and my bodie I commit to the earth to be buryed in the north chapel of the parish church of the aforesaid East Bridgford: Item I give to my sonne Francis Hacker my eldest sonne three hundred pounds of lawful Englishe monie: Item I give to my sonne John Hacker my second sonne one hundred pounds of like lawful Englishe monie: Item I give to Rouland Hacker my third sonne one hundred pounds of like lawfull Englishe monie: Item I give to Richard Hacker my youngest sonne one hundred pounds of like lawfull Englishe monie: Item I give to John Wighteman my daughter Elizabeth her sonne twenty pounds: Item I give to my said daughter Elizabeth and the rest of her children to be divided amonge them at her discreson Foure score pounds: Item I give to my daughter Marie Daye thirtie pounds: Item I give to my daughter Luce Meafeild twenty pounds: item I give to John Hacker my sonne Francis his eldest sonne five pounds & to evrye one of the rest of my sonne Francis his owne children fourtye shillings a peece: Item I give to Anne Hacker my sonne John Hacker his daughter five pounds and to evrye one of his other children fourtye shillings a peece. Item I give to evrye one of the children of my sonne Richard Hacker fourtye shillings ... Item I give to John Mafeild my daughter Luce her sonne five pounds: Item I give to Margaret Raggesdale my said daughter Luce her daughter five pounds: Item I give to Mearie Mafeild my said daughter Luce her daughter fourtye shillings: Item I give to evrye one of my daughter Luce her other children not before named fourtie shillings a peece. Item I give to the poore of East Bridgford five pounds to be distributed to them at the discresion of my sonne Francis Hacker and my sonne Rouland Hacker: Item I give toward the repayre of the church of East Bridgford three pounds: item I give towards the making of a tomb for my selffe and my deceased husband tenne pounds. Item I give to my sonne Francis his wife Margaret Hacker my daughter in law a peece of gold of the value of *xxi* Item I give to Barbara Hacker my sonne Roulands wife of a peece of gold of the like value: I give to Edward Good my nephew xx ii: Item I give to my daughter Elizabeth Harpar my daughter Mearie Daye and my daughter Luce Meafeild all those diamons which I bought of my sonne Francis Hacker ... lye in a ... of my said sonne Francis in the chamber over the kitchen to be equally divied amongst them: Item I give to Elizabeth Rossell ... daughter a cubbord with a presse ... which ... in the kitchen: Item I give my biggest gold ringe to my daughter Elizabeth Harpur: Item I give to daughter Barbara Hacker my gold ringe worth foure guineas Item I give to my daughter Luce my ringe worth three guineas: Item I give to my daughter Marie my ringe which is poesie Gods providence is my inheritance ... ... of my goods not yet ... by this my last will my debtors paid and my funeral expense discharged my will is that there bee equally devided amongst all mye children ... Francis Hacker John Hacker Rouland Hacker Richard Hacker my sonnes Elizabeth Harpar Mearie Daye Luce Meafield my daughters. And I make Francis Hacker my sonne executor of this my laste will and testament ... Margarett Hacker

Money Equivalents			
1628	**2022**	**1628**	**2022**
21s	£219.70	3 guineas	£659.00
22s	£230.10	4 guineas	£878.70
40s	£418.40	£30	£6,276
£3	£627.60	£80	£16,740
£5	£1,046	£100	£20,920
£20	£4,184	£300	£62,760

"Items of furniture were expensive and often passed through generations as treasured items alongside tableware and linen. The prices below are taken from the book *Early 17th-Century Prices and Wages by Hugget and Peachey.* Their sources were mainly household accounts and probate inventories amongst others."

FURNITURE PRICES IN THE EARLY TO MID 17TH CENTURY

Cupboard with press - £1 13s 4d *(approx. £348.80 in 2022)*

Other cupboards varied from 5s -16s *(approx. £52.30 - £167.40 in 2022)*

Chests varied from 2s 6d - 13s 4d *(approx. £26.15 - £139.50 in 2022)*

Chairs varied from 2s -16s

Couch £2 *(approx. £418.40 in 2022*

FRANCIS HACKER I

17 August 1640

Proved 20 May 1647 Prerogative Court of Canterbury

In the name of God Amen I Francis Hacker of Colston Basset in the County of Nottingham Esquior this seventeenth day of August in the Sixteenth yeare of the Raigne of our Soveraigne Lord King Charles Anno Domini One Thousand Six Hundred and fortie being of perfect mind and memory thanks bee to God but weake in bodie considering that all men must die but that non one knows the time of death and for that it is the Duty of every Christian to settle peace and quiet by a timely disposition of such wordly goods as it hath pleased God to blesse him with doo ordaine and make this my Last Will and Testament hereby revoking and makeing void all former Wills And first I bequeath my Soul unto the Maker and give thereof God the father Son and Holy Ghost three persone but one God believing and trusting to bee saved by the onelie merits of Jesus Christ my onely Saviour and Redeemer And I appoint my Bodie to bee buried in the parish Church or Chappell of East Bridgeford nigh unto my late wife And for my worldlie Goods I doo hereby dispose of them as followeth That is to saie I doo give and bequeath unto the poore of the Parrish of East Bridgford Forty shillings of lawfull English money to bee distributed att my Buriall Item I give and bequeathe unto the poore of Colston Basset Forty shillings of like lawfull English to be disposed of as aforesaid And for my Lande Tenemente and hereditaments I dispose of them as foloweth. Whereas I have a sonn called Richard my oldest sonn whom I knowe not whether hee bee living or dead but being minded to dispose of my Lande Tenemente and hereditaments from him in Case hee should bee living I doo therefore hereby bequeath and give unto my Sonn Francis Hacker All that my house Lande Tenemente in Colston Bassett with their and everie of their appurtenances To have and to hold the said house lands tenements and hereditaments to him the said Francis Hacker his heries and assignes for ever Item I give and bequeath unto my Sonn Thomas Hacker All that my house Lande Tenemente and hereditaments lying in Bridgford to have and to hold the said house lande tenemente and hereditaments to him the said Thomas for and during his natural life and after his decease to the heirs Males of his Bodie lawfully begotten or to bee begotten and for Default of such issue to remaine and come to mee my heires and assignes for ever Item I give to my Sonn Rowland Hacker Twenty Pounds per annum of lawfull English money out of my Lands tenements and hereditaments on Kinholton to bee paid unto him by even and equall portions att the two most usuall feasts of St Michaell the archangel and the Annuntiation of the Blessed Virgin Mary the first payment to begin the first of the feasts Daies which shall first happen next after my Decease. And as for my personal Estate of Goods and Chattels I doo hereby dispose of them as followeth my Debts being paid I give and bequeath unto my daughter Ann Six Hundred Pounds of lawfull English money too bee paid to her within three months next after my decease for her Portion and childs part Item I give unto my daughter Alice Grocoke the summe of One Hundred Pounds of lawfull English money to bee paid unto her within Three Months next after my decease for her portion and childs part Item whereas I stand ernsted by Nicholas Stirley for George Stirley his sonn with the Reciepts of part of the proffits of ceartaine Cole Mynes lying in Stirley and Bilborough in the County of Nottingham for and during the Minority of him the said George Stirley and to and for the onelie use and benefit of him the said George Stirley I doo hereby appoint and ordayne my Executor or Executors hereafter named to pay all such sommes of money unto him the said George Stirly att his age of One and Twenty years as shal be made to appear to have been received by mee. And for the Remainder of my Goods and Chattels my Debts and Legacies being paid and performed and my funeral charges discharged I doo hereby give and bequeath unto all my children equally to bee divided and distributed *betwixt them (in side margin)* and amongst them and I doo ordayne and appoint my son Francis Hacker and my sonn Thomas Hacker the sole executors of this my last Will and Testament Witnes my hand and seal which I have hereunto sett The Day and yeare above written Francis Hacker Signed Sealed published and delivered as the Last Will and Testament of mee Francis Hacker in the presence of Henry *Pekham* Roger Jackson Clerke Richard *Rowse* his mark John Southwicke

Money Equivalents			
1640	**2022**	**1647**	**2022**
40s	£379.40	40s	£302.40
£20	£3,794	£20	£3,024
£100	£18,970	£100	£15,120
£600	£113,800	£600	£90,730

When calculating the equivalent money values in 2022, it was interesting to see how the value dropped considerably between 1640 when Francis wrote his will and 1647 when it was proved.

SHOPPING LIST
ARMING A SOLDIER

Cuirass (breast plate) with pauldrons (shoulder plates)	£1 6s
Cuirass without pauldrons	£1
Lance armour	£4
Target of proof (shield)	24s
Armour of proof (suit of musket-proof armour)	£14
Repairing one helmet	1s 6d
16ft pike	£4
Matchlock musket	10s 6d
Bandoleer of gunpowder	22d

FRANCIS HACKER III

Written 1685

Proved 5 June 1694 Prerogative Court of Canterbury

In the name of God Amen I Francis Hacker of the Towne and County of the Towne of Nottingham gent. being of perfect sound and disposeing mind and memory and in a good state of health thanks be to Almighty God yet considering that I am naturally borne to dye and the great uncertainty of humane life and how frequently men are surprized by an unexpected and sudden death and my mind and intention is hereby to order and dispose of such estate as it hath pleased God to afford me therefore I make this my last Will and Testament in manner and forme following that it is to say first and principally I commend my soule into the hands of Almighty God my Creator and of his sonne Jesus Christ my only Saviour through whose mercy and meritts I doo assuredly hope to obtaine pardon for all my offences and to inherit the joys and fruition of eternall life My body I commit to the earth to be decently buryed at the discretion of my Executors hereafter named Whereas I the said Francis Hacker have had and received a considerable porcõn with Anne Hacker my dear and beloved wife amounting to the summe of three hundred pounds and upwards and have not made any jointure or settlement of Lands or Tenements upon the said Anne or any other provision for her support and maintenance if she happen to survive me and to the infant she may have a competent subsistence after my decease I doe hereby give bequeath and devise one Messuage or Tenement with the appurtenances situate and being in Statherne in the County of Leicester with all barnes stables buildings gardens orchards yards barbsides wayes commons profitts and comodities to the said messuage appertaining or there with enjoyed and one Croft or Close thereunto adjoyning and one halfe Oxgange of Land thereunto belonging and therewith used or enjoyed and alsoe two Leas of ground and a Wind Mill thereupon standing And also our Hose called the Hall Hose containing about foure acres with their appurtenances lying and being within the Libertyes and Precincts of Statherne aforesaid unto my said wife Anne Hacker for and during the terme of her naturall life and afterwards to the heires of the body of me the said Francis Hacker on the body of the said Anne lawfully begotten or to be begotten and for defan... or want of such issue to the ... Heires of me the said Francis Hacker forever And for the enabling of my said Wife to pay all my just debts which shall be oweing by me at the time of my decease and for the maintenance and duration of my children and alsoe for the paying and discharging of my funeral expenses I give and bequeath all my goods chattells and personall estate whatsoever unto my said Wife Whom I make my full and sole executrix of this my last Will and Testament And my will mind and meaning is that after the decease of my said Wife if the aforesaid Messuage Lands and Premises shall descend and come unto Francis Hacker my eldest son or in case he shall dye before my said wife and the said Messuage and premises shall descend or come to any other my children which I now have or hereafter shall have by Anne my said Wife That he she or they to whom the same premises shall come or descend shall pay his or their younger brothers and systers and the survivors or survivors of them the summe of thirty pounds apiece to each of them as he she or they shall severally attaine unto their respective ages of one and twenty years And in case any of them shall dye the parte or porcõn of him her or them soe dyeing shall goe and be paid unto the survivors or survivors of them equally to be divided amongst them share and share like And alsoe my mind and will is that the said Messuage Lands and Premises shall be lyable thereunto and chargeable with the payment thereof in witness whereof I have hereunto sett my hand and seale the nine and twentyeth day of June in the first yeare of the reigne of our Sovereirgne Lord King James the second ... Anno Domini one thousand six hundred and eighty five Francis Hacker Signed sealed and published in the presence of ... Athorpe Joseph Turpin ... Knight

Money Equivalents			
1685	2022	1694	2022
£30	£4,872	£30	£4,640
£300	£48,720	£300	£46,400

SAMUEL HACKER

Written 13 September 1722

Proved 18 April 1724 Prerogative Court of Canterbury

In the Name of God Amen the thirteenth day of September in the year of our Lord God one thousand Seven hundred twenty and two I Samuel Hacker Citizen and haberdasher of London being of Sound and perfect mind and memory God be praised do make and ordane this my last will and testament in manner and forme following (that is to say) first I commend my Soul into the hands of Almighty God my mercifull Creator hoping and stedfastly believing to obtain everlasting life through the precious and meritorious Death and sufferings of my Lord and Saviour Jesus Christ and my body to the Earth to be decently buryed at the discretion of mine Executrix herein after named. Item Whereas in and by certain Articles of Agreement in Writing Indented Tripartite bearing date the one and thirtieth day of March in the tenth year of the Raigne of our late Soveraigne Lady Anne late Queen of Great Britaine ... Anno ... Domini 1711 made or mentioned to be made betweene me of the First part Samuel Crompton then of Derby and now London Gentleman of the second part and my now wife Elizabeth (by the name of Coape Widow. Relict of Henry Coape late of Duffield aforesaid ... deceased) of the third part I have Covenanted and agreed to lay forth four thousand pounds in purchasing Lands Tenements or Hereditaments of as great a yearly value as can be conveniently got for the Same and to convey and settle the Same or cause the Same to be conveyed and Settled in manner and to certaine uses and purposes in the Said Articles mentioned and in and by the Said Articles I have farther Covenanted and agreed that in case I dye before such Intended purchase and Settlement Shall be made that then my Heirs Executors and Administrators Shall pay to my aforesaid Wife the yearly Sume of two hundred pounds in manner as therein is Expressed untill Such Said Intended purchase and Settlement Shall be Soe made as aforesaid now therefore I hereby doe for and in full Satisfaction of the Said Articles and of all the Covenants and agreements therein give and bequeath to her my said aforesaid Wife the Sume of four thousand pounds of lawfull money of Great Brittaine to be by her Raised had and taken as Shall be most Convenient from and out of all or any of the Severall Shares Estate and Interest which I have or Shall have in all or any of the Severall Capitall or principall Stocks or Funds of the United Company tradeing to the East Indies commonly called East India Stock not hereby otherwise disposed of the Governor and Company of the Banke of England and commonly called Banke Stock not hereby otherwise disposed of and the Stock or Fund of the Company of Shipmakers or from and out of all or any other part or parts of my Estate reall or personall not hereby otherwise disposed of in Trust and to the Intent that she my said Wife her Executors or Administrators may and shall with all Convenient speed bestow and lay forth the Same in purchasing Lands Tenements or Hereditaments of as great a yearly Value as can be conveniently got for the Same and may and Shall Convey Settle and Assure or raise to be Convey'd Settled and assured such said Lands Tenements or Hereditaments when so purchased in Such Manner and to and for Such uses intents and purposes and Subject to Such provisions and Agreements as in and by the said Articles are and is mentioned limitted directed or appointed So far as the deaths of partyes will admitt of and from time to time until Such Said Intended purchase Shall be Soe made all the Interest and produce to Arise and be made of and from the said four thousand pounds is to goe and be paid to Such person and persons and in the Same manner as the Rents and profitts of the Said intended purchase would goe and be paid in case such Lands Tenements or Hereditaments soe intended to be purchased weresoe purchased and settled as aforesaid and such said Interest and produce to be taken and accepted by my Said Wife for and in full Satisfaction of the aforesaid two hundred pounds per Annum soe covenanted as aforesaid to be yearly paid unto her till such Said intended purchase and Settlement Shall be soe made as aforesaid Item Whereas I have Already given with my daughter Dorothy a Fortune or portion on her marriage with Mr. Giles Sadler I doe now hereby further give unto her the sume of two hundred pounds of lawfull money of Great Britaine to be paid unto her within Six Kalendar Months next after my decease Item I give and bequeath to my daughter Elizabeth Hacker fifteen hundred pounds Interest or Share in the aforesaid Capitall Stock or fund of the Governor and Company of the Banke of England commonly called Banke Stock and also five hundred pounds Interest or Share of and in the Capital or principall Stock of the Governor and Company of Merchants of Great Brittaine trading to the South Seas and other parts of America and for encourageing the Fishery commonly called South Sea Stock. Item I give and bequeath unto my daughter Hannah Hacker two thousand and two hundred pounds Interest or Share in the Capitall or principall Stock or Fund of the United Company Tradeing to the East Indyes commonly called East India Stock when and if she shall live and attaine her age of one and twenty years or be married which of them shall first happen and if it shall happen that my said daughter Hannah shall dye before She Shall attaine her said age of one and twenty years or be married then and in such case my aforesaid Wife is to have and Enjoy to her own use all the Annuall Dividends and profits of those said two thousand and two hundred pounds East India Stock from and after the decease of my said daughter Hannah for and during the Term and unto the full end and Term of five years from thenne next ensuing and fully to be compleat and ended if She my Said Wife Shall so long live and at and after the end or other *determination* of the Said Term of five years then I give and bequeath the said two thousand and two hundred pounds East India Stock in manner following (that is to say) one Thousand pounds Stock part thereof to my aforesaid daughter Dorothy Sadler and twelve hundred pounds Stock Residue thereof to my aforesaid daughter Elizabeth Hacker Item I do hereby make Nominate Constitute and appoint the aforesaid Elizabeth my Wife to be the Sole and only Executrix of this my last will and Testament and for the Enabling my said Executrix to pay my debts and the Legacies by me hereby given and my Funeral expenses and for the *perfor* manner of this my Will I give devise and bequeath unto my said Wife and Executrix and to her Heirs Executors and Administrators and assignes forever all my Shares Estate and Interest which I have or Shall have in all or any of the aforesaid Capitall Stocks or Funds of the united Company tradeing to the East Indies the Governor and Company of the Banke of England the Governor and Company of Merchants Tradeing to the South Seas and other parts of America and for encourageing the Fishery and Company of the Shipmakers aforesaid and all my goods Chattells debts owing unto me and Reall and personal Estate whatsoever (except what are or is hereby otherwise disposed of by me) and my mind and will is that when all my debts and Funeral Expenses and the *Legaties* by me hereby given and all charged Expenses and payments in and about the Execution of this my will and he Trusts therein or any way collating thereto and fully satisfiyed and paid the thereafter Residue of all my Estate both reall and personal Shall go remaine and be unto and to the onely use and behoofe of the aforesaid Elizabeth my Wife her Heirs Executors Administrators and Assignes forever Item I doo hereby Revoke all former Wills by me herefore made in Witness whereof to this duplicate of this my last will and Testament containeing three whole sheets of paper and soe much as is Written on this last Sheet I have to every of the said sheets set my hand and to the First and last Sheets I have set my Seale the day and year First before written Saml Hacker Signed Sealed published and declared by the before named Samuel Hacker the Testator for and as his last will and Testament (the word Tripartite being underlined in the First Sheet and the words if She my Said Wife Shall so long live and he words or other *determination* being underlined in the third sheete) in the presence of us who all Subscribed our names as Witnesess hereunto in the presence of the said Testator John Baddeley Hugh Bateman Thomas Stevenson

A codicil was written date 4 January 1723

H Codicill to be annexed to the last will and Testament of Samuel Hacker Citizen and Haberdasher of London Whereas the Said Samuel Hacker have in and by my last will and Testament in Writing bearing date the thirteenth day of September one Thousand Seven hundred twenty and two given unto my daughter Dorothy the Wife of Mr Giles Sadler the sume of two hundred pounds of lawfull money of Great Brittaine to be paid unto her within Six Kalender months next after my decease now my mind and will is that the said Legacy or Sum of two hundred pounds Shall cease and not be paid and that my Said daughter Dorothy Shall have and I doe hereby give and bequeath unto her my Said daughter Dorothy in how and Stead thereof two hundred pounds Interest or Share of and in the Capitall or principall Stock of the Governor and Company of Merchants of Great Brittaine trading to the South Seas and other parts of America and for encourageing the Fishery commonly called South Sea Stock and Whereas I have in and by my said last will and Testament given and bequeathed to my daughter Elizabeth Hacker (inter alia) Five hundred pounds Interest or Share of and in the Capitall or principall Stock of the Said Governor and Company of Merchants of Great Brittaine trading to the South Seas and other parts of America and for encouraeging the Fishery commonly called South Sea Stock now my mind and will is that two hundred pounds Interest or Share part of the said five hundred pounds Interest or Share of and in the said Capitall or principal Stock of the Said Governor and Company of Merchants tradeing to the South Seas and other parts of America and for encoureaging the Fishery Shall not goe or accrew to my Said daughter Elizabeth and that she my said daughter Elizabeth Shall have onely three hundred pounds Interest or Share part of the said five hundred pounds Interest or Share of and in the Said Capitall or principall Stock of the Said Governor and Company of Merchants tradeing to the South Seas and other parts of America and for encoureaging the Fishery over and besides the Fifteen hundred pounds Banke Stock given her by my said Will and Whereas I have in and by my Said last will and Testament given to my daughter Hannah Hacker two thousand and two hundred pounds Interest or Share in the Capitall or principall Stock or Fund of the united Company tradeing to the East Indyes commonly called East India Stock when and if she shall live and attaine the age of one and twenty years or be marryed which of them shall First happen and if she dye before She Attaine that age or be marryed then the same and the profitts thereof go to or be disposed of in manner as in my Said Will is mentioned now my mind and will is that in case my Said Daughter Hannah Shall Marry before She Shall Attaine her age of one and twenty years without the approbation and consent of my aforesaid Wife that then and in such case She my Said Daughter Hannah Shall have and take by my Said Will only one Thousand pounds Stock part of the Said two thousand and two hundred pounds East India Stock so thereby given unto her as aforesaid and my mind and Will farther is that my wife may at any time after my decease have power to Sell and convert the Said two thousand and two hundred pounds East India Stock or any part or parts there before the Same Shall be payable and disposable of hereby or by my Said Will into ready money and that the money arising by Such Sale and the Remainder (if any) unsold of the Said Stock and the Interest and profitts thereof Shall go and be applyed in *Hie..* Stead and Satisfaction of all the Said Stock to Such persons and in such manner as the said whole two thousand and two hundred pounds East India Stock and the profitts thereof would have done in case the same of any part thereof had not been Sold and I doe hereby direct that this Codicill be annexed to my Said last will and Testament and be attopted as part thereof in Witness whereof to this duplicate of this Codicill I have put my hand and Seale the fourth day of January Anno Domini one Thousand Seven hundred twenty and three Saml Hacker Signed Seales published and declared by the within named Samuel Hacker for and as a Codicill to be annexed to his last will and Testament within mentioned and for and as part of his Said Will in the presence of us who all subscribed our names as Witnesses hereunto in his presence

Josiah Rogerson Hugh Bateman John Roe

Money Equivalents	
1724	2022
£200	£33,190
£300	£49,780
£500	£82,970
£1000	£165,900
£1200	£199,100
£1500	£248,900
£2200	£365,100
£4000	£663,800

FRANCIS HACKER IV

Written 8 October 1715

Proved 17 March 1716 London

In the name of God Amen I Francis Hacker of White Fryers London Gent doo make this my last Will and Testament in manner following (Viz) My soul I recommend to Almighty God my maker in hopes of Salvation through the merits of our ever blessed redeemer Jesus Christ, As to my body I leave it to be buried to the discretion of my Executrix, And as to my personall Estate I doo hereby give and bequeath the same to my Loveing Mother Anne Hacker whom I hereby constitute and appoint my Sole Executrix, And as to my Lands and Hereditaments in Statherne my Will and mind is and I doo hereby devise the same to my said Mother for and during her natural life, And I doo hereby give her being well and in good health within two years after my decease in full power and authority to charge and raise out of the rents Issues and profits of the said Lands and Hereditaments in Statherne aforesaid the sume of fifty pounds for her own use by Mortgage and otherwise, Paying all my just debts (Viz.) To an Apothecary in Fleet Street Six Shillings To Paschall Tennant thirty odd shillings, to Mr Staples Hatter and the Bookseller at the flower de Lure in Fleet Street London Half a crown each And I also give to my Sisters Anne Dunton and Elizabeth Lynch a Guinea a piece to buy them a Ring

Signed Sealed Published and declared by the said Francis Hacker to be his last will and testament this eighth day of October One thousand seven hundred and fifteen

In the p... Of those who signed the same in the Testators p...

Elizabeth Lynch

Dinah Williams

Edw. Wood

John Steer

Money Equivalents	
1716	2022
2s 6d	£19.87
6s	£47.69
Guinea (21s)	£166.90
30s	£238.50
£50	£7,949

ROWLAND HACKER I

I April 1639

Proved 9 May 1639 Nottinghamshire

In the name of God Amen. I Rowland Hacker of East Bridgford in the County of Nottingham gent being sicke in body but of sound and perfect memory doo ordayne and make this my last will and testament the first day of Aprill the fifteenth yeare of the reign of our most gracious Souovraigne Lord Charles by the grace of God of England Scotland France and Ireland King Defender of the Faith ... ... manner and forme following First I give and commit my soule into the hands of Almighty God my heavenly father steadfastly trusting though his almighty power and the merits amd martyrs of Christ Jesus my Saviour and redeemer to be found among the ... and chosen of God and my body I commit to the earth from whence it ... to be buried in the north Ile of the church of East Bridgford aforesayde near unto my former wife deceased And for my wordly goods with God in the greate mercy hath ... me I dispose thereof as followes Iuprimis I give towards the repayre of the Church of East Bridgford aforesayde ten pounds of lawfull mony of England and I desire the Rector of the said Church for the time being and his successors and the churchwardens successively to see that the said tenn pounds be imployed to the best use and that the use arising from it be bestowed yearly (or as occasion shall serve) upon the repayres of the sayde church and to have an offetiale case that the said ten pounds nor any parte thereof be lost nor impaired Item I give and bequeath to the pore of East Bridgford aforesayde ten pounds of lawfull money of England to be payde unto the Churchwardens and overseers of the poore and to be by them imployed to the best use and my will is that the use hereof be by him imployed for the putting forth of poore children apprentices such as shall be borne in the towne of East Bridgford aforesayde and I desire the Rector of East Bridgford for the time being and his successors and the Church Wardens and overseers of the poor successively to have an esspetiall ... that the sayde ten pounds nor any parte hereof be lost or wasted Item I give and bequeath unto William Boscastle and his children in satisfaction of all wrongs and trespasses done unto him one peece of medow which he hath in Little Jug in the parish of Car Colston for the space of three years next ensuing the date thereofe Item I give unto Alice King my servant one Cow or ffiftie shillings in mony and the Cottage house with the appurtenances hereunto belonging wherein Andrew Kinge her father now dwells for by and during all the term of my lease ... and paying therefore yearely unto ... executor the yearly Rent of twenty six shillings and eight pence of good and lawfull money of England and I desire ... Executor hereafter named that they may have the sayde Cottage house and the appurtenances thereto belonging upon the sayd rent during her natural life. Item I give my servant John Caunt six shillings and eight pence and to my servant Thomas Ball five shillings and to the rest of my servants two shillings six pence a peece Item I give and bequeath my grand ... Roger Walldrom my best Silver Salte and by best Silver Boule and one fowling peece and Burding peece

Rowland Hacker

Money Equivalents			
1639	**2022**	**1639**	**2022**
2s	£17.97	26s 8d	£239.60
5s	£44.93	50s	£449.30
6s	£53.91	£10	£1,797

ROWLAND HACKER II

3 June 1673

Proved 28 June 1675 Nottinghamshire

In the name of God Amen ... in the five and twenty the Raigne of our Soveraigne Lord Charles the ... England Scotland, France King Defender of the faith And in the year of our Lord ... One thousand Six hundred and ... three I Rowland Hacker of East Bridgford in the County of Nottingham Esq of good ... and Sound memory praised ... Almighty God therefore Doo ... this my last Will and testament in manor and forme following First ... to Almighty God, being fully ... by his holy spirit through the ... Death and .... Jesus Christ to obtaine full pardon and confession of all my Sins and to inherit every ... And my body to be buried in the North Quire within the parish church of East Bridgford aforesaid according to the discretion of the overseers of this my last Will and testament hereafter mentioned And for my worldly Goods this I bestow ... I Give and bequeath unto Charles Hacker my First son all and singular my lands tenements and heriditaments whatsoever with thappurtenences lying and being within the Fields and territorys of East Bridgford aforesaid to have and to hold immediately from and after my decease to him and his heirs forever (except one Cottage Lease of one cottage and one close thereunto belonging called or known by the name of *Spencors* Wong lying in Bridgford aforesaid now or late in the tenure of Thomas Sponge or his assigns I give and bequeath to my son Ferdinando to have and to hold immediately from and after my decease to him and his heirs for ever And I give and bequeath to my said son Charles Hacker ... my lands Tenements and hereditaments lying and being in Kinoulton in the said county of Nottingham with all and singular thappurtenences to have and to hold to him and his heirs for ever paying and discharging all and singular such legacies as hereafter in this my Will is ... Item I give and bequeath to son Ferdinando the sum of three hundred pounds to be paid by my son Charles Hacker out of my Estate in Bridgford and Kinoulton within six months after ... said Charles shall come to the possession of the same But if it pleases God that my said son Ferdinando shall dye before the said Legacy of three hundred pounds shall ... be paid. Then my will is that Two hundred of the said three hundred pounds shall ... to my son Charles and the other one hundred pounds to be paid to my daughter *Mary* and my daughter Sarah Brough equally to be divided betwixt them. Item I give a... to my daughter Mary Westby the sum of Fifty pounds ... son Charles within Six months after he shall ... to y... to my daughter Sarah Brough the sum of *five* shillings ... within ... after my decease Item I make and ordain my Son Charles Hacker executor of this my last Will and testament And my dear friend ... of Ratcliffe Esq and John Jackson of Burton in the County of Nottingham ... this my last will and testament. And I give to each of them the ... For their pains... in... ing them in the name of God to see that this my last will and testament may be pformed accordingly. And I utterly revoake all former Will and Testaments by ... made or declared. In witnesse whereof I have unto sett my hand and Seale this day and year above written ### Rowland Hacker ### Read Signed and Sealed & delivered ... to be my last will & testament in the presence of
Charles Grant John Trewman Jo: Sherwood

Money Equivalents	
1673	2022
£300	£50,830

This next will is one of the most interesting and fascinating wills I have ever read and transcribed. Apart from the obvious wealth Francis possessed, the detail of his bequeathments gives a wonderful insight into the contents of a 17th-century household, albeit a rich one, and equally the family relationships involved within. Despite two of his daughters being alive at the time of writing, Anne aged about sixteen and Lucy about fifteen, only Lucy is well taken care of. Daughter Lucy is given a substantial Portion (Dowry) the equivalent today being about a quarter of a million pounds, half of which daughter, Anne, only receives if Lucy dies.

Perhaps in the 17th century, there was a logical explanation for this.

There is a possible marriage for Lucy to Henry Tate of St Paul, Shadwell, Middlesex on 19 July 1685 at St Katherine Cree, London. It was a year after her father died and she would have received her inheritance.

I have been unable to locate marriage records for Francis's children, Ann, Dru or William, but it might be that the records have not survived. Just as a reminder, Francis is the brother of William Hacker, the merchant who was murdered in Frankfurt in 1651.

FRANCIS HACKER (SALTER)

17 August 1684

Proved 20 October 1684 Prerogative Court of Canterbury

The last will and testament of Francis Hacker of London Salter now living in Houndsditch in the parish of Buttolph Algate the seaventeenth of August Anno incarnatianis et redentionis Christ Salvator M..... 1676 I say one thousand six hundred seventy and six

In the name of God Amen

1. I doe give and bequest to my loving wife Anne in ... of her joynture and thirds one hundred pounds ster. per Annum to be secured to her as shee shall like best out of my Land in Yorkshire and out of my Lease at Cardigan in Wales. I say one hundred pounds per Annum during her life being soe agreed upon with her Brother Deane before marryage

2. I doe give unto my said wife if shee doe content herselfe with the one hundred pounds per Annum for her joynture and Thirds I doe give her all my silver Plate and Spoons besides excepting one silver Tankard one silver Poringer and two guilt spoones which I give to Daughter Lucy and two silver Trencher Salts otherwise to sell them and add the pr... to the personall Estate

3. Alsoe I doe give unto my said Wife the best Bedd with the Curtaines Vallens Hangings of the Roome Chairs Stooles and all other appurtenances belonging to the said Chamber and a Pallate bed for her Maid to lye upon

4. It. I doe give me Wife all and all kind of Linen except two pr. sheets and Pil. I give to Lucy with one dozen of Napkins which are in being in the house at the time of my death

5. It. I doe give her all the Pewter in the House excepting two doss: of Plates and one other Dish of each size of the Pewter Dishes which I give unto Daughter Lucy with two Pewter Porringers and two Pewter Kandlesticks and one Brasse

6. It. I give said wife two brass Kettles and a Skillett and two brasse Candlestick And to Daughter Lucy one Brasse Kettle and Skillet and to sell the rest

7. I give my Wife her Clossett with all things belonging to it silver and Pewter neither intended as to belong to her Closett

8. For Iron tongs Shovells And irons … pr. lett Wife and Daughter Lucy take what they like and will use and sell the rest

9. What is mentioned above is given to my Wife is with the condition that she doe accept of her one hundred pounds per Annum joynture and wholly renounce her Thirds and that if shee doe insist upon her Thirds whether she … the same or not by Law then my will is that shee shall have none of the things above mentioned to be given her but that all and everything shall be sold excepting what is given as above to Daughter Lucy to the best advantage to augment the Estate Moreover. I give to Daughter Lucy above what is exprest amongst her Mothers Viz^t one quart silver Tankard one silver porringer two guilt spoons and two silver Trencher Salts two paire of Holland Sheets and two paire of Pillowbeers and one doss: of Napkins of the best (excepting my Wifes Damaske) It. two dozen of Pewter trencher plates and one single Pewter Dish of every size (whereof I think there are six sorts yet if there be but one of a sorte of some of the sorts then Wife to have that her selfe two pewter Porringers five pewter Candlesticks and one brasse Candlestick one brasse Kettle and brasse Skillet one paire of iron shovell and Tonges Iron Doggs all of moste of these things being inserted amongst her all others is my will Lucy shall have and enjoy but through … mentioned this last mentioning of them being but a varite all of them together which were disperst amongst her Mothers before shee shall not have double but single what is before mentioned but besides them things I doe give to Daughter Lucy one serge Bedd wherein her Mother and I did most usually lye with all the Bedding Viz^t feather bed Mattris Bed under it Pillowes two, Bolster one white Rugg two Blankets Counterpaine with Curtains and Vallens Cupboard Cloth two Chairs two or three Stooles all the same Style and unto the said Bedd and Chamber belonging Alsoe I doe give her the Pewter Cisterne the Pewter Bason and Stand all at present made use of and in the said Chamber Alsoe I give said Lucy one Spanish Table and a little Trunke in my Closett Alsoe I doe give unto Daughter Lucy fifteen hundred pounds ster. for her portion to be paid her out of the personall Estate when she arrives at the full age of Twenty years and doe advise her not to marry before then and in the intrim I doe give her Thirty two pounds per Annum for her dyett and cloathing and to live with her Mother I doe alsoe advise her and board where shee board or I advise her to live at her Uncle Tindalls or at her Coss: Bowater or at her Uncle Hackers at any of which places I suppose she may be boarding at twelve pounds per Annum And it is my will that she shall not marry to any without her Mothers consent and good likeing and that in case shee doe before shee receives her portion shee shall then receive but one thousand pounds instead of the one thousand five hundred pounds and the rest to be divided in thirds to her Mother and two Brethren William and Dru Hacker but if she doe not marry until shee be twenty years old then shee shall have the whole one thousand five hundred pounds paid her and it shall be wholly at her dispose after if she dye a Maid to give it to any of her Kindred but doe advise especially to have respect to her Brethren or to pious uses but if shee dye before shee be twenty years old then her one thousand five hundred pounds to be divided betwixt her two Brethren William and Dru

10. It. I do give to my Wife the Persian Carpett and two Spanish Tables my money chest and … Boy of Drawers in my Closett and two Leather Carpetts and one dozen of the best Turkey worke Chaires It. I doe give my Daughter Lucy the Turkey Carpett a Leather Carpett and all the other Turkey worke Chairs and Stooles being as I think eleven or twelve of them And for my Land in Yorkeshire which I bought of Thomas Best at Hoxton in Cleaveland in Yorkshire And also that other land which I bought

of Sr Robt Layton lying in Sutton juxta Dugby in Cleaveland in Yorkshire being about a mile from Hoxton I give to Sonne Dru during his life and to his Children after him forever but not to have possession of it untill he attaine the age of Thirty yeares but after he is twenty six yeares of age then I order that hee shall receive Thirty pounds per Annum untill hee be full thirty years of age It. I doe give to Sonne William that Lease of Land I bought of George Ludson who bought it of James Phillips of Cardigan in Wales I say that Lease of Land lying in about and neare Cardigan aforesaid hee paying off all the Kings Rent which is about fifty Pounds per annum and Mr ?andy for his life forty pounds per annum and too Priests one tenne pounds per Annum and thith.^r fifty shillings or sixty shillings per Annum and alsoe except my Wifes joynture to be paid out of it being one hundred pounds per Annum I doe give him the said Lease with all the profits during his owne naturall life excepting as before excepted but not to enjoy it or put in possession of it untill hee be fully thirty years of age yett when he arrives to twenty six years of age untill hee come to Thirty I give and allow him Thirty pounds per Annum to maintaine him but when hee comes to be in possession of the ~~~ Lease hee shall have not power to sell the same but only to rec. the cleare profits whilst the Lease lasts or his owne life and after to his Children and if not Children then to his Brother Dru and his Children And if Dru dye without Children Then I give his Land to his Brother William and his Children and if both dye Childlesse then I give both the Land and Lease to their Sister Lucy and her Children and if shee faile of Children Then I give it to the next of Kindred Hackers brother J^{no} Hackers younger Sonnes and Brother William Hackers two Daughters the Daughters to have halfe soe much as the Sonnes It. I give to Sister Knight to my Cozen Jane Brigham and her sone Hacker Brigham each of them gould mourning Rings of Twenty Shillings a piece value. It. I give to my two Niece Hackers my Brother Wm Hackers Daughters each of them one silver Tankard of Tenne Pounds value a Tankard and two gold mourning Rings of Twenty shillings piece each of them. It. I doe give to our two Maid Servants Mary and Katherine five pounds a piece to each It. I doe give and bequeath to Sawley in Darbyshire the Towne of my owne and Mothers Nativity the summe of Two Hundred pounds ster. the profitts whereof I doe only intrust them withall until they shall or doe find out a convenient purchase to lay out the money upon and then at least three or foure of the ablest men of the Towne Copy holders or ffree holders shall engage soe much of their Lands to make good the principall and pay out the profitts according as I doe intend and whilst they faile I doe intend to lodge the said in the hands of the Worshipful Company of the Salters of London and for the first five yeares they only receive forty shillings per Annum to be distributed at every Christmas to some of the poorest Women and Men of the said Towne but after the five years and in which I presume a stock of fifty pounds will be raised besides the two hundred pounds principall which I doe alsoe give unto the aforesaid Towne of Sawley to buy fflax ... ... or Woole to make Linnen Cloath or to make woollen or Worsted Stockings whereby the poorer sorte of people by Spinners and Knitting may be kept in continuall worke and receive such dayly or weekly wages for their worke done as may sustaine them and keepe them from the dolenesse (and begging the fruits thereof) but if the Townes men shall be soe poore spirited that they will not give good security to maintaine the saide Poores ... of fifty pounds without the least diminution of the principall from yeare to yeare and infinitis then I doe give order and appoint the said fifty pounds to be added to the first two hundred pounds to make it up two hundred and fifty pounds and to be also paid in unto the aforesaid Worshipfull Company of Salters hands in London takeing their Bond for the same with their Hall seale to it for confirmation (as is their custome to repay the principall with the Comon Interest which is now six pounds per ... per Annum And at the end of five years when the fifty pounds is raised and in readynesse for a stock if the Towne doe accept it on the terme proposed to them then the twelve pounds Interest yearly arising I doe give this to buy Tenne ... of Tenne Shillings a poire price all gray cloth to be given yearly to Towne poore people that are least able to worke where of six Women and foure to be Men and Tenne paire of new shoes of two shillings a paire and ten paire of new Stockings of eighteen pence a paire and ten new shirts and smocks of two shillings a piece and four shillings six pence in Pitt roales to each of Tenne poore people which I think will by a Carte Load to each if the Townes men will be soe charitable to fetch then home for them and all and everything to be given and distributed to them every Easter or Whitsuntide And forty shillings per Annum I doe give to some good Schoole master or Schoole Mistresse to teach the poorer sorte of peoples Children to read English without any pay from them. It. If the Towne men of Sawley doe not accept of the fifty pounds stock ... is above the proposed then my will is it shall be added to the two hundred pounds first mentioned to make it two hundred and fifty pounds principall the profits whereof I doe give as above and for the Poore of the Towne of Sawley in manner as is above exprest but for the distribution of the Interest of the fifty pounds if added to the two hundred pounds will be three pounds per Annum my will then further is that every of the Tenne poore People shall receive two shillings a piece in money every Christmas and every Easter two shillings apiece alsoe and shall add to their Pitt roales two shillings each ... more to make up the foure shillings sixpence for roales to be six shillings and sixpence to each and every one of them It. My will is that Brother Jn° Tindell Jn° Hacker Cozen Jn° Bowater do Anunni ... upon the Estate and are desired to advance it what reasonably they may until the time limited when they are to receive their several Portions and to pay them such allowances as is before mentioned and if they see it reasonable them to choose some particular wise and discreet man to negotiate matters for them and shall every halfe yeare render them a true and just ... of all his actings of receipts and payments and to give him such salary as the judge reasonable And for Brother Tindall Brother Hacker and Coss. Bowater I doe give them Tenne Pounds each man for undertaking the trouble and for their paines besides allowances for their contingent and necessary expenses from time to time Dated twenty sixth of August one thousand six hundred seventy six /Francis Hacker/ signed and sealed in presence of Nichols Lanton ... Underhill

EXAMPLES OF ITEMS FROM THE WILL

SILVER PORRINGER
17TH CENTURY

PEWTER PORRINGER
17TH CENTURY

"It might be useful to point out that early Pewter had a very high lead content, thus eating and drinking from these vessels would cause the lead that leached out to be absorbed by the body, causing many deaths from lead (pewter) poisoning. The lead was removed from later pewter manufacturing processes."

17TH-CENTURY PEWTER CANDLESTICKS RIGHT

Once again, we see the value of the pound has dropped between 1676 and 1684

Money Equivalents							
1676	2022	1676	2022	1684	2022	1684	2022
2s	£18.07	£10	£1,807	2s	£16.88	£10	£1,688
4s	£36.13	£12	£2,168	4s	£33.76	£12	£2,026
4s 6d	£40.65	£32	£5,781	4s 6d	£37.98	£32	£5,402
6s	£54.20	£100	£18,070	6s	£50.65	£100	£16,880
10s	£90.33	£200	£36,130	10s	£84.41	£200	£33,760
20s	£180.70	£250	£45,170	20s	£168.80	£250	£42,200
40s	£361.30	£300	£54,200	40s	£337.60	£300	£50,650
50s	£451.70	£1000	£180,700	50s	£422.00	£1000	£168,800
60s/£3	£542.00	£1500	£271,000	60s/£3	£506.50	£1500	£253,200
£6	£1,084			£6	£1,013		

THOMAS GOODE

22 May 1580

Proved 20 June 1580 Prerogative Court of Canterbury

In the name of God Amen the two and twentie day of May in the xxi[th] yeare of the raigne of our Soveraigne lady Elizabeth by the grace of god of England France and Ireland Quene defender of the faith … And in the yeare of our Lord god 1580 I Thomas Good of Abington in the Countie of Cambridge visited and afflicted in bodie through sicture but of good and perfecte remembrance thanks to god my maker therefore doe institute and ordeine this my last Will and testament in manner and forme following first as my soule and spirite is to be preserved before all other things noherewith god hath endowed me I take care of the same first and especially comitting and resigneing the same into the hands and protection of my mercifull god and almighty creator in the mediation of his Christ by whome I have assurance through faith in his merritts to be an inheritor of the everlasting kingdome of heaven next I commit my body to the yearth to be buried in the churchyard of Abington in such solemye and decent order as is posed amongst Christtians Item I give to Clemens my wife all that she brought and twentie pounds in ready money to be paid within one yeare after my death Item I bequeath unto the said Clemens two and fiftie shillings out of my land at Wendye to be paid during her natural life Also I will that she have a chamber tenne years her boarde the saide tenne years providing herewith all that in case my said wife and my sonne William shall not live peaceably together ether through disturbance of his or her parte or his wife if yt chance him to marrye that then if my said wife shall thinke it convenient to departe that for so many years as shall remaine after her depture my sonne shall paie her twenty shillings yearly until the tenne years be expired Item I give to my eldest sonne William the Lease of my farme at Abington during tenne years after my death And it is herewith a condicion that he shall bringe up my three children Edward Henry and Grace during those tenne years at learning providing them all things necessary also at the terme of tenne years ended he shall leave the same farme to Edward and Henry my sonnes with all such furniture as is at this … belonging to the same he shall leave the land sowen and filled as he entreth of yt. Item I give and bequeath unto my sonne John all that Thomas Lechworth oweth me Item I give unto my saide sonne John twentie royles of sheep at hatlie and tenne pounds in money besides item I give unto my sonne Richard threescore pounds Item I give unto Francis my sonne my house at Bassingbourn during the space of tenne years furnished discharging the Lords rent and at the end of the said tenne years to leave all things furnished as he findeth them Item I bequeath unto the said Francis all my mault at Bassingbourne and [Foiston] and at (?ixes) Item I give to the said Francis twentie acres of land wth I bought of [Ashewell] Item I bequeath unto my daughter Margaret tenne pounds Item I give to my daughter Mary fortie pounds two bease twentie shepe and a chamber furnished Item I give unto my daughter Grace fortie pounds two beast twentie shepe and a chamber furnished Item I give and bequeath unto the church of Abington tenne shillings Item I give to the poore of the same parishe ten shillings Item that in case it shall please god to call out of this life any of my children to whome these goods are bequeathed that theire porcon shalle be equally devided amongst the surviurs In conclusion I do ordeine my sonne William my sole executor and do appointe Thomas Batt of Abington one of the witnesses unto this my last Will and testament the … of my will to see all things therein specified are duely executed in every respecte and in recompense of his paines I give him tenne shillings … William Cragge Clerke John Hinton and Thomas Batt being present with the departed person in his visitation when he was of good remembrance doe witness according to his request that this is his true last will and testament

Money Equivalents	
1580	**2022**
10s	£171.80
20s	£343.60
52s	£893.30
Royl (15s)	£257.70
£10	£3,436
£40	£13,740
Three Score Pounds (£60)	£20,620

ELIZABETHAN SHOPPING LIST

Good Shirt	£1
Pair of knitted socks	15s
A good pair of boots	£6
A coat	7s 2d
A loaf of bread	2d
A quail	1d
A chicken	1d
Beef	4d a pound
Butter	3d a pound
Bottle of French wine	2s
A tankard of ale	1/2d
Lodging at an Inn (with laundry)	2d per week
Tobacco	12s 50d per pound
A small book	7d

APPENDIX II

VISITATION OF NOTTINGHAMSHIRE
1662-1664

HACKER OF FLINTHAM

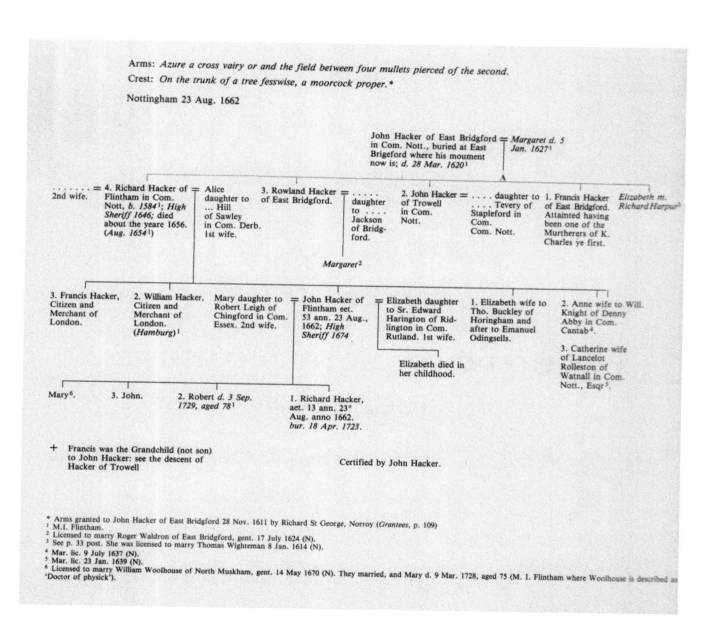

Arms: *Azure a cross vairy or and the field between four mullets pierced of the second.*

Crest: *On the trunk of a tree fesswise, a moorcock proper.* *

Nottingham 23 Aug. 1662

John Hacker of East Bridgford = *Margaret d. 5* in Com. Nott., buried at East *Jan. 1627[1]* Brigeford where his moument now is; *d. 28 Mar. 1620[1]*

A

...... = 4. Richard Hacker of = Alice
2nd wife.   Flintham in Com.   daughter to
              Nott, b. *1584[1]; High* ... Hill
              Sheriff 1646; died   of Sawley
              about the yeare 1656. in Com. Derb.
              (*Aug. 1654[1]*)   1st wife.

3. Rowland Hacker = ...   2. John Hacker = ... daughter to   1. Francis Hacker   *Elizabeth m.*
of East Bridgford. daughter   of Trowell   .... Tevery of   of East Bridgford. *Richard Harpur[3]*
                   to ....   in Com.   Stapleford in   Attainted having
                   Jackson   Nott.   Com.   been one of the
                   of Bridg-   Com. Nott.   Murtherers of K.
                   ford.   Charles ye first.

Margaret[2]

3. Francis Hacker,   2. William Hacker,   Mary daughter to   John Hacker of   Elizabeth daughter   1. Elizabeth wife to   2. Anne wife to Will.
Citizen and   Citizen and   = Robert Leigh of = Flintham eet. = to Sr. Edward   Tho. Buckley of   Knight of Denny
Merchant of   Merchant of   Chingford in Com. 53 ann. 23 Aug., Harington of Rid-   Horingham and   Abby in Com.
London.   London.   Essex. 2nd wife.   1662; *High*   lington in Com.   after to Emanuel   Cantab[4].
                     (*Hamburg*)[1]   *Sheriff 1674*   Rutland. 1st wife. Odingsells.
                                                                                                                          3. Catherine wife
                                                                               Elizabeth died in   of Lancelot
                                                                               her childhood.   Rolleston of
                                                                                                                         Watnall in Com.
                                                                                                                         Nott., Esqr[5].

Mary[6].   3. John.   2. Robert *d. 3 Sep.*   1. Richard Hacker,
                            1729, aged 78[1]   aet. 13 ann. 23°
                                                     Aug. anno 1662.
                                                     bur. 18 Apr. 1723.

+ Francis was the Grandchild (not son)
  to John Hacker: see the descent of   Certified by John Hacker.
  Hacker of Trowell

---

* Arms granted to John Hacker of East Bridgford 28 Nov. 1611 by Richard St George, Norroy (*Grantees*, p. 109)
[1] M.I. Flintham.
[2] Licensed to marry Roger Waldron of East Bridgford, gent. 17 July 1624 (N).
[3] See p. 33 post. She was licensed to marry Thomas Wighteman 8 Jan. 1614 (N).
[4] Mar. lic. 9 July 1637 (N).
[5] Mar. lic. 23 Jan. 1639 (N).
[6] Licensed to marry William Woolhouse of North Muskham, gent. 14 May 1670 (N). They married, and Mary d. 9 Mar. 1728, aged 75 (M. I. Flintham where Woolhouse is described as 'Doctor of physick').

HACKER OF TROWELL

Arms: *Azure, a cross vairy or and of the field between four mullets pierced of the second.*

Crest: *On the trunk of a tree fesswise, a moorcock proper.*

Nottingham 25 Aug. 1662

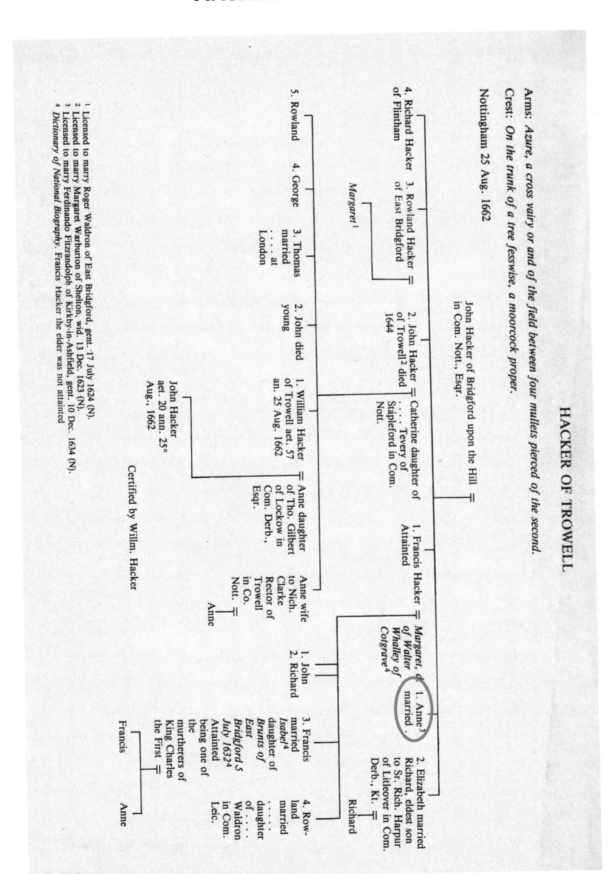

John Hacker of Bridgford upon the Hill in Com. Nott., Esqr.

Certified by Willm. Hacker

1 Licensed to marry Roger Waldron of East Bridgford, gent. 17 July 1624 (N).
2 Licensed to marry Margaret Warburton of Shelton, wid. 13 Dec. 1623 (N).
3 Licensed to marry Ferdinando Fitzrandolph of Kirkby-in-Ashfield, gent. 10 Dec. 1634 (N).
4 *Dictionary of National Biography.* Francis Hacker the elder was not attainted

77

APPENDIX III

THE HEATHCOTE HACKER VAULT

One theory as to the resting places of our Hacker family members lies in the Heathcote Hacker vault under St Peter's Church, East Bridgford. The stone pictured below is located on the north side of the church, almost in line with the wall monument inside. Although they were a much later branch of the family, the vault could have been dug out earlier with room for future burials and the stone erected at later date by the Heathcote Hackers. All quite plausible. However, this theory was thrown to the wind when Lynne Black of the East Bridgford History Society kindly sent a newspaper article dated 22 May 1965. the headline…

Family Burial Revealed

East Bridgford Vicar Examines Seven 19th Century Coffins

Seven lead coffins between 154 and 75 years old made an unexpected reappearance in the 13th century St Peters Church, East Bridgford, on Sunday.

A five foot square stone-slab sealing the entrance steps of the burial vault of the Heathcote Hacker family collapsed. It gave the vicar, the Rev. Victor Johnson, an unexpected opportunity to examine the interior of this large family vault situated beneath the site of the church's former north transept, demolished in 1778.

Brass plaques

He found five leads coffins resting on the stone floor, a sixth bricked up and sealed off in the north-east corner and a seventh in a brick-lined cavity beneath the floor slabs.

And all bore commemorative brass plaques. The coffins were those of the Rev. Edward Heathcote, who died on April 7, 1811, aged 82; Ann Hacker, died June 10, 1830, aged 62; Ralph Hacker, died February 3, 1841, aged 70; John Heathcote Hacker, died October 16, 1870, aged 76; Roeland Heathcote Hacker, died October 6,1885, aged 51; and Agnes Heathcote Hacker, died March 3, 1890, aged 83.

The Old Hall, East Bridgford, was the home of the Hacker family for nearly four centuries until 1925.

But the vault was not open for long. Workmen are at present engaged on fabric repairs on the church roof and within 12 hours the vault had been resealed. "It is unlikely ever again to be disturbed." says the vicar.

Little would he have known that forty-six years later, an archaeological evaluation of St Peter's church would be undertaken in 2011, and the vault was once again examined.

N.B. The Rev. Edward Heathcote died 7 April 1801, not 1811. Also, it was Ralph Heathcote, not Hacker, who was buried in the vault.

HEATHCOTE HACKER VAULT

A report written in February 2011 by Andrew Failes BA (Hons) MA on the *Archaeological Evaluation at St Peter's Church, East Bridgford, Nottinghamshire*, describes the work undertaken for Inclusive Designs Limited.

Lynn Black also kindly provided a copy of the report and said the survey was carried out when there were plans for an extension to the church.

A most interesting part of the report was the investigation of the Heathcote Hacker vault.

Page 9 - Records show that the north transept was demolished in 1778 (Du Boulay Hill 1932, 120) and although a construction cut for the vault structure was not recorded (probably due to its being obscured by stone revetment in Trench 5), the north wall and ceiling of the vault clearly stand proud above the former church floor, suggesting that the vault was built post 1778 after the transept was demolished. The presence of the alcove at the eastern end of the vault confirms this, as it was constructed where the wall and foundation of the former transept would have been.

Examination of the inside of the vault with a borescope revealed that the brickwork of the walls was probably the same as that of the barrel vaulted ceiling. Plate 13 shows the internal south wall of the vault and the vault ceiling.

The borescope survey was able to confirm most of the 1965 newspaper report describing the contents of the vault. The article describes seven lead coffins, five resting on the stone floor, the sixth in a bricked up alcove and the seventh in a brick lined cavity beneath the floor slabs. The coffin underneath the floor slabs could not be observed as the slabs had been relaid, but the five coffins resting on the floor are shown in Plate 14, while Plate 15 shows a hole knocked through into the bricked up alcove with a coffin resting on the ground inside. The survey also identified a large stone plinth constructed against the internal north wall (Plate 14). The purpose of this structure is unknown but its existence raises the possibility that another coffin might be located within the plinth itself.

"The evidence shows that the vault was made late 18th - 19th century, many generations after the Hackers of interest in this study."

VIEW INSIDE VAULT LOOKING WEST SHOWING 5 LEAD COFFINS
Image reproduced with the kind permission of the East Bridgford History Society

APPENDIX IV

PORTRAIT OF FRANCIS HACKER II

COLONEL FRANCIS HACKER
OWNED BY CHARLES MALCOLM-BROWN - FIG. 1

The images featured are reproduced with the kind permission of Charles Malcolm-Brown and have an incredibly interesting backstory.

The painting (Fig. 1) was said to be Colonel Francis Hacker when Charles purchased it from an antique dealer in Norfolk, and this declaration led to his determination to prove its authenticity. By tracing three previous sales, it was tracked back to 2018 when it was sold at Lawrences Auctioneers, Crewkerne, Somerset and described as having been painted by a follower of Edward Mascall from c.1627 to c.1675. It was thought to be a portrait of Francis III, however, research proved that this was not so.

JJ Heath-Caldwell is related to Samuel Hacker, Colonel Francis's youngest son, through marriage, and a wealth of information relating to his numerous ancestors can be found on his website. He saw the portrait and alerted the auctioneers to an almost identical painting (Fig. 2) that had been sold at Nye and Company Auction House, New Jersey, USA, in 2009. Its size being 29 x 23 inches. This one had the name Col. Hacker written top left and was sold by a man from Rhode Island, USA, said to be a picker/dealer. Unfortunately, no other information could be provided.

The art expert at Lawrences Auctioneers, Richard Kay, suggested that both of these paintings might be copies of an original.

The painting in Fig. 1 was cleaned and restored by Alison Porter from Cambridge. She thought that the canvas weave aligned itself with the 17th century, although she questioned whether the cloth of the canvas might have come from abroad, perhaps the USA. She also thought it might have been cut down from a larger oval portrait whose origin and location are unknown.

The style of the costume was confirmed by the Bath Fashion & Textile Museum as being from the 1640s or later, which would have put Francis in his thirties or forties when the portrait was painted, and around the time when the English Civil War broke out.

There is also further information that helps identify these paintings as Francis II…

COLONEL FRANCIS HACKER
SOLD IN THE USA - FIG. 2

Until the discovery of these two paintings, the only popularly known image of Francis was an engraving held at the National Portrait Gallery (NPG D20296). Although the costume was identified as being from the 1650s, again by the Bath Textile & Fashion Museum, this line engraving was produced a hundred years after Francis's execution. Thanks to Charles's diligent research, the N.P.G. has since retitled it as: *unknown man engraved as Francis Hacker.*

Many thanks to Charles Malcolm-Brown for providing the information featured in this Appendix. Further thanks to Charles are expressed for generously loaning the newly discovered portrait to the National Civil War Centre, Newark, Nottinghamshire from 25th May 2024.

Further research connected to these paintings has revealed that a portrait of Colonel Francis Hacker was displayed at the First Special Exhibition of National Portraits at the South Kensington Museum, in April 1866. This painting was loaned by Earl Cathcart, and its description reads:

Republican Soldier of Fortune; much trusted by Cromwell and his party; had custody of the King during his trial, and led him on to the scaffold; at the Restoration he was tried, and executed at Tyburn, 19 Oct. 1660

Bust; buff coat, white collar. Oval, canvas, 29 x 23.

The same size as the one sold in the USA.

Then, in the book Memoirs of the Martyr King - by Allan Fea et al, published in 1905, appears a portrait almost identical to Figs. 1 & 2, and is listed as being in the possession of Lord Cathcart. The slight differences in this particular portrait could suggest it might be the original painting from which the copies were made.

THE BUFF COAT

The buff coats featured in the paintings were made from oil-tanned hide and lined with linen. They could provide some protection from swords and edged weapons, but not firearms and were worn under armour.

Francis Hacker's buff coat also resides at the National Civil War Centre and is on loan there from the Royal Armouries Museum, Leeds. The description on their website tells us that the coat was bought by Hearst, an American businessman in 1936, probably William Randolph Hearst, at the Fenton sale. This would be William Henry Fenton

(1864-1936) who lived at Heston House, Heston, Middlesex. He was a curiosity dealer in London.

Further details include that it was thought to have been the property of Lord Cathcart, related by marriage to Hacker. According to the correspondence file, at the time of the sale, there was a note to say that the Cathcart family still had a picture of Hacker wearing the coat, and Fenton states that it <u>was</u> purchased from Lord Cathcart.

There is also a reference to the Hacker buff coat on the Connoisseur stand at the Antique Dealers Fair and Exhibition in London, in June 1953.

THE HACKER/CATHCART CONNECTION...

Samuel Hacker's second wife was Elizabeth Coupe neé Crompton (see page 36). Her great nephew, Sir Samuel Crompton, married Isabella Sophia Hamilton Cathcart in 1829. Their daughter, Elizabeth Mary Crompton, married Alan Frederick Cathcart (1828-1905) the 3rd Earl Cathcart, in 1850. He was most likely the Lord Cathcart who owned the painting of Francis Hacker and his buff coat.

The painting was still with the Cathcart family in 1936, but its whereabouts now is unknown.

COLONEL FRANCIS HACKER
OWNED BY LORD CATHCART

APPENDIX V

LETTER WRITTEN ON 4 JUNE 1660 BY MARGARET FELL

LETTER WRITTEN ON 1 JANUARY 1661 BY ISABELL HACKER

LETTER WRITTEN ON 4TH JUNE 1660

This letter appears to be a short note written by a mother to her children and reveals her concern regarding the somewhat precarious position Colonel Francis Hacker and Colonel Axtell found themselves following the Restoration of King Charles II.

The letter is signed with the initials M F, who is possibly Margaret Fell, a founder of the Quaker movement. She was known as the 'mother of Quakerism'.

Letter reproduced with the kind permission of Paul Clarke

TRANSCRIPTION

London the 4th of the 6: mon 1660

Deare & eternally beloved Lambs & babes of God my deare

love in the everlastinge fountaine flowes forth freely unto

those who are deare & neare unto me even as my owne

life, never to be forgotten in that ever lastinge bond of love

& unity. my deare loves dwell & keepe where our life is

hidd with … in god the God of love be *your* everlastinge

strength for ever. I am in hast & soe I cannot en-

lardge. I expect that G: F: should be heare some

tyme the next weeke, but yet I have not heard

how they have *proceeded* as in order to his bringing

up hither. the Act of Indemnity is not yet per-

fectly past, but this day the two houses hath sat

in a grand Comittee & it is sayd that Collo. Hacker

& Coll: Axtell is left out of the Act as intendes to

suffer, befiles :7: of the Kings Judges that is the most

your Brother is in health he was herewith and this day

An downer & Mary Sanders is this day sett for-

wards towards the North with G: Robts & Gobort Sykes

which two last doth intend to returne with G F if he

come for London Thus in short I rest with my

deare love in the *Lords* to all friends

Your Deare mother

M: F:

my deare love is dearly

remembered to the …

to Friends H: F:

G F is probably George Fox

TRANSCRIPTION OF A LETTER WRITTEN BY ISABEL HACKER ON 1 JANUARY 1661

The 1st of the 11th month 61: [1st January 1661]

Deare Friend A D

My deare love, with deare Michell & Francis & Mary flowes mightily to thee & thy deare Husband, yea more & … … can stop it nor set bounds thereto: for it is boundless in which we reach to each other over that head that would devid us; oh! the Infinit depths of this love, wisdome & power of our god, who in this glorious appearing of his day which is Rissen & appeared, to fill the empty, poore & hungery lambs that cannot be satisfied with any thinge short of that *true* … that came downe from god, but the Rich & full sends empty away, glory, glory, glory everlasting be unto the god of all life onely.

ah! My deare friend, my love to thee & the deare husband is both knowne by & in the feeling life in which we are united together forever: oft have deare Francis & I desired to see thee in this place, if it were the will of the lord, in which is our rest & Content, but yester day being the third day of the weeke, did deare JP meete at the Bulls mouth, to take his leave of Friends: & our thoughts run much to RD & thy selfe where our hearts desired that you might then feele what was felt by the lambs of the true fould here.

Oh! How did the glory of our god Cover the earth & his bowells melt the hearts of his before him: truly it was a glorious meeting as ever I was at & I beleive [sic] the souce of that love which flowed from, & burst out Ran over in the Chosen Vessell will not easily be lost; & G.W. sat by exceeding still. I never saw a fuller meeting in that place. But the day before JP desired to meet with the Bretheren that were his Elders or before him in the truth & did at GR house wher was G.F. F.H: R.H: GW mett him. And Michell, John Osgood, John Peniman, Francis, Mary Booth & my selfe & Robert Cobit who was accidently there, but was not desired; all was set for some time in silence, & then JP prayed, & spoke in the pure cleer life & power of gods bowells of love & did desire that the bretheren would freely let their loves go a long with him & did … god onely, & lay the creature in the dust before him: which was hard to be borne; as by one oppssion, which I may hint, which was this in the very words to the best of my Remembranns. JP did declare that the most learned had dayly need of the teachings of god: at which some did startle as it were & Replyed that was to make Ignorant Repeating it severall times, by this thou may savor of the rest. But JP being *thou* v…dor an obligation told them that he could not then stay longer in that Respect; yet nevertheless, they prest him to stay much espeially [sic] RH, & said, John then seems to desire our love, then stay, at which JP in much Tenderings said keep it for me till to Morow & promised to meet them the next day about the second house (after the meeting at the mouth) at Will: Travers house & the same Company to be there, which was accordingly; onely Willyam Pennington & Edward Bellnig [sic] was added, Edwards comenig [sic] was not thought on till he *cam in*: & when all was set in stillness RH begane to Repeat the former discorse of JP the day before, & lengthened it much with divers Agravations; so when he was silent JP said, he had a long discorse to answer & it might be possible that his memory might faile him; & therefore desired that if he did miss in any pticuler, they that heard it would helpe him therein, by reminding him of it. So he began with the first & so to every pticular of the discorse: Truly deare Ann the god of Eternall power wisdom & love did mightily appeare in his Tender lambe, whose liveing Testimony for god to my understanding (& all who came not with a prejudice against John, or any of them) as Clear as Christiall; & they seemed to be something Coole at last, all except RH. But the Germanie doctor & his wife, and some others coming into the Roome Caused a Riseing at present. But they went with JP into an upper Roome, & then RH showed as I heard more bitterness: & spoke hard things, which I shall forbeare to wright: but when thou comes thou will heare the full Relation of the truth of it, but GF & FH & GW *pted* in love with him & so did deare Will: Dewsbury (who is well) & H:J:

This day JP depted this City & had a meeting at Acton, where he lyes this night, and RW. hath got liberty For some time to stay forth, he intends to go a long a while with him; he is to be at Gads?en the 6th day wher a meeting is to be; Mary Stanclife & Sarah Wooldrig, prissilla & I, intende if the lord will to be there; we go to *Talvornes* in the Coach & then walke the 6th miles from there. On the 7th day John passes to Isaac Penningtons where he stayes 10 day or more: & then onto towards Bristole, & so for Ireland; I know not of any that goes with John to Ireland, saveing one J Browne a deare old friend of Johns. Deare Friend I do believe god hath made him feele thy sufferings for him, he did oft speak in deep bowells of thee, in which he did express that thou was exceeding deare unto him, he hath left something with us, to be coppyed out for thee, & he hath left something with me, which None can give thee but myself. Thou may gess what it is all our loves is to you & Friends in the truth ther a wayes

Dear Ann I am Thine   Issible Hacker

AD is Ann Downer

Francis is possibly Francis Howgill

JP is probably John Pennyman

Bulls mouth – The Bull & Mouth was a 17th-century inn in London

Bellnig is Edward Belling

Gads?en – tentative guess could be Godstone

Talvornes perhaps means Taverns?

Mary Stanclife is possibly the wife of Michael Stanclif to whom Isabel's son, Samuel, was apprenticed

Speaking in deep bowells could derive from the bowels being traditionally regarded as the seat of tender and sympathetic emotions; from the bowels of mercy - Oxford Reference

APPENDIX VI

TRANSLATION OF DOCUMENT E178/6285
NATIONAL ARCHIVES

DOCUMENT E178/6285 NATIONAL ARCHIVES

Inquisition as to the possessions of Henry Smith and Francis Hacker, attainted.

12 January 1661

Indented inquest taken at the Borough of Leicester in the said County on the 29th day of January in the 12th year [1661] of the reign of our lord Charles the Second by the grace of God King of England Scotland France and Ireland defender of faith etcetera, Before William Streete esquire, William Ireland gent, and George Palmer gent, commissioners of the Lord the King by virtue of a commission of the same lord the king directed to the same commissioners and others and attached to this inquest, by the oaths of Thomas Tompson of Belgrave gent, John Tooley gent, Thomas Tompson of Glenfield gent, George Hubbard, John Fisher of Belgrave, Thomas Wells, Robert Cooper, Thomas Smalley, Roger Waldram, Humfrey Smalley, John Steedman, Thomas Steedman, John Avery, Francis Pawley, William Mould, William Marshall, John Fisher of Cossington, William Burrowes and Richard Whattaph ^esquires^ approved and lawful men of the said county, who having been sworn and charged, upon their oaths say that Henry Smith Esquire (named in the said Commission) on the 25th day of March in the year of the lord 1646 (specified in the same Commission) and afterwards was seised, and still is seised, of and in the Manor of Wythcott alias Wythcocke with appurtenances in the said county of Leicester, and of and in the advowson of the parish church of Withcott alias Withcocke aforesaid, and of and in one chief messuage with appurtenances called the Mannor House, and of and in one other messuage with appurtenances called the Viccaridge house, and of and in two cottages with appurtenances called Shepheards houses, and also of and in nine hundred acres of arable land, meadow and pasture with appurtenances in Wythcott alias Wythcocke aforesaid, in his demesne as of fee, of the annual value in all issues after deductions of six hundred pounds. And furthermore the said jurors say upon their said oaths that the said Henry Smyth on the 11th day of February in the year of the lord 1659 [1660] mentioned in the said commission and afterwards at Wythcott alias Wythcocke aforesaid was possessed of one hundred ewe sheep, in English ewe sheepe, and one hundred lambs worth 66 pounds 13 shillings and 4 pence, which were afterwards sold by the said Henry Smith to various persons now unknown to the same jurors and the moneys arising therefrom were paid to a certain Roger Smyth esquire, brother of the said Henry, and to William Money a servant of the said Henry Smyth or one of them, and also that the said Henry Smith aforesaid on the 11th February in the last aforesaid year, at Withcott alias Wythcocke aforesaid had been possessed of three horses or mares or geldings, six cows, and four oxen, worth seventy pounds, which four oxen were afterwards sold by the said Henry Smith to a certain William Tarrey of Gilsborough in the county of Northampton yeoman, for the sum of thirty pounds, and also the said three horses and six cows were likewise afterwards sold by the said Henry Smith to various persons now unknown to the said jurors and the moneys arising therefrom were paid to the said Roger Smith and William Money or one of them, and also that the said Henry Smyth aforesaid on the 11th day of February in the last aforesaid year and afterwards at Wythcott alias Wythcocke afroresaid was possessed of twenty other sheep called weather hoggs worth 13 pounds 6 shillings and 8 pence, and of twenty other sheep called ewe hoggs worth 10 pounds , and that the said twenty sheep called weather hoggs were afterwards sold by the said Henry Smith to various persons now unknown to the said Jurors, and the said twenty sheep called ewe hoggs were afterwards sold by the said Henry Smyth to a certain Francis Chamberlayne of Tilton in the said county of Leicester gent for ten pounds, and the moneys arising both from the said sheep called weather hoggs and from the said other sheep called ewe hoggs were afterwards paid to the said Roger Smyth and William Money or one of them, and that the said Henry Smith after the said 11th day of February in the year of the lord 1659 [1660] (specifed in the said commission) namely on the second day of May in the year of the lord 1660 at Wythcott alias Wythcocke was possessed of sixteen acres of barley in sheaves, twenty six acres of oats in sheaves, and five acres of rye in sheaves, growing in certain several fields or pastures of the said Henry Smith called Ash Hill, the great Rough closse and Castle Hills in Wythcott alias Wythcocke aforesaid, which several acres of barley, oats and rye aforesaid were afterwards namely on the said second day of May in the last aforesaid year sold by the said Henry Smith to a certain Thomas Swan of Loddington in the said county of Leicester yeoman, for the sum of eighty pounds, and the moneys arising therefrom were paid to the said Henry Smith, and also that the said Henry Smith on the said 11th day of February in the year of the lord 1659 [1660] aforesaid and afterwards at Wythcott alias Wythcocke aforesaid was possessed of various goods and chattels following namely one waggon, in English a waggon, and of certain seats and chairs, called in English stooles and chayres, to the value of five pounds, which goods and chattels last mentioned afterwards by the delivery of the said Henry Smyth came into the hands and possession of a certain John Prettyman of Loddington in the said county of Leicester knight and baronet and still remain in his hands, and also that the said Henry Smith on the said 11th day of February in the year of the lord 1659 [1660] aforesaid and afterwards at Wythecott alias Wythecocke aforesaid was possessed of two geldings worth twenty five pounds, which geldings were afterwards sold at Wythcott alias Wythcocke by the said Henry Smyth to Lady Elizabeth Burton of Stockerson in the said county of Leicester widow and the money therefrom arising was paid to the said Henry Smith.

Francis Hacker Esquire on 25 March 1646 was seised of and in one messuage and two acres of land with appurtenances in Stathern in his demesne as of fee, of the clear annual value of 20 shillings, and also possessed of and in one messuage and eighty acres of land meadow and pasture with appurtenances in Stathern for the term of several years thereafter to come, now or late in the tenure or occupation of Edward Shephardson Esquire of the clear annual value of forty pounds.
Francis Hacker was also after the 11th February 1659 namely on 1 May 1660 at Stathern possessed of 350 sheep worth £175, some of which were sold to John Rynill of London, butcher, others were sold to Edward Gardner of Burton in Leicestershire gent, and the money arising was paid to Isabella Hacker wife of Francis Hacker, and the rest of the sheep to the number of ninety were seized by William Hartopp of Dalby parva Leicestershire for rent due in arrears from Francis to William.
Also Francis Hacker on 1st May last past at Stathern was possessed of one gelding worth 80 shillings which was seized by William Hartopp for rent due. Also Francis Hacker on 1st May last at Stathern was possessed of nine heifers worth each forty shillings, which were afterwards sold by Francis Hacker to William Hande of Oakham in Rutland and the money arising paid to Isabella Hacker wife of Francis Hacker.

Translation and summary of document E178/6285 from Latin was kindly carried out by Peter Foden.

Acknowledgements

- Special thanks to Philip Yorke for his continuing support and encouragement
- Special thanks to Steve Wells for the front cover image and illustration page 18
- Special thanks to Julie Penaluna for the illustration page 30
- Special thanks to Sean Gallagher
- Staff at the Nottinghamshire Archives
- Jayne Hoare at Cambridgeshire Archives
- Staff at Nottingham University Manuscripts and Special Collections
- Staff at the National Archives
- Peter Foden - consultant
- Jonathan Ferguson - Leeds Royal Armouries Museum
- Lynne Black - East Bridgford Local History Group
- Dr Richard Allen - Magdalen College Oxford University
- Felix Lancashire - Royal College of Physicians
- Katie George - The Salters Company
- Charles Malcom Brown for finding the portrait of Francis II
- J J Heath-Caldwell for knowing of the existence of Samuel Hacker's portrait
- Lord Charles Cathcart - the 7th Earl Cathcart

Sources

Books and Documents

- Some Account of the Hacker Family - by E. Lawson Lowe F.S.A - Old Nottinghamshire - edited by John Potter Briscoe 1881
- Colonel Francis Hacker - parliamentarian and regicide - by H. Leslie Hubbard, 1941
- The story of an English Village - Arthur du Boulay-Hill
- Deposited Documents - Nottinghamshire Archives
- Thoroton's History of Nottinghamshire Volumes I and II
- Hearth Tax 1664 & 1674
- Transcripts of Archdeaconry Trials - Nottinghamshire Archives
- The Visitation of Nottinghamshire 1662-1664 - made by William Dugdale *Norroy King of Arms* Edited by G.D. Squibb, L.V.O., Q.C., F.S.A.
- Memoirs of the Life of Colonel Hutchinson - by Lucy Hutchinson
- The Journal of George Fox - from Internet Archive Digital Library
- Clarke's Papers - Online Library of Liberty
- Marriage Law for Genealogists - by Rebecca Probert
- Reading Old Handwriting - by Eve Mc Laughlin
- Archaeological Evaluation at St Peter's Church, East Bridgford, Nottinghamshire, 2011 by Andrew Failes BA (Hons) MA
- The Constables Accounts of Stathern - transcribed and edited by Everard L Guilford M.A
- The Churchwardens Accounts of Stathern 1630-1677 - transcribed and annotated by the Rt. Rev. F J Western M.A
- Sir Thomas Stanhope of Shelford - by Beryl Cobbing and Pamela Priestland
- Lords Journals, XI. 101. In extenso - National Archives Main Papers
- Village Life in Tudor and Stuart Times - A study of Radcliffe-on-Trent - Edited by Pamela Priestland and Beryl Cobbing
- Memoirs of a Martyr King - being a detailed record of the last two years of the reign of His Most Sacred Majesty King Charles the First (1646-1648-9) - Allan Fea et al - Google Books in public domain
- East India Company Coat of Arms: By This W3C-unspecified vector image was created with Inkscape . - Own work, based upon [1], CC BY-SA 3.0, https://commons.wikimedia.org/w/index.php?curid=15648243

Websites

- findmypast.co.uk
- ancestry.co.uk
- measuring worth.com
- Manuscripts and Special Collections, University of Nottingham
- Nottinghamshire Archives Worldwide Catalogue
- The National Archives
- Royal College of Physicians - history.rcplondon.ac.uk
- Wikitree.com
- quod.lib.umich.edu (Trial Transcript)
- www.nottshistory.org.uk
- www.eastbridgford-history.org.uk
- www.southwellchurches.nottingham.ac.uk
- www.bottesfordhistory.org.uk

Index

About the Author

Catherine Pincott-Allen has a passion for history and loves nothing more than delving into the past to uncover the truth about long-forgotten people and events.

Catherine is a founding member of The Field Detectives, an East Midlands-based group of history enthusiasts that use the latest technologies to prove, or disprove, historical theories. In addition, she's also a devoted family historian and can regularly be found at local county records offices poring over census, probate and property records.

A Further Account of the Hacker Family is Catherine's fourth published book. Her first book, the novel *Gloria*, was published in 2021 using the pseudonym Emmaline Severn. In the same year, her *Richard Thomas Parker* biography - about the last man to be publicly hanged in Nottingham - was also published. Also, in 2024 she published a short story *Steady as She Goes* - the poignant wartime memories of a WWII navy 'medic'.

Catherine is based in the East Midlands, where she lives with her husband, Richard.

READER REVIEWS

Critical praise
for the author

'A new view point
on history'
☆☆☆☆☆

'An absorbing,
unputdownable
read'
☆☆☆☆☆

'Had me hooked
on the turn of
every page'
☆☆☆☆☆

'A thoroughly
enjoyable and
compelling read'
☆☆☆☆☆

'Wonderful story,
brilliantly told'
☆☆☆☆☆

Milton Keynes UK
Ingram Content Group UK Ltd.
UKHW051119210424
441235UK00004B/24